HMH | (into) Math™

Volume 1

Modules 1–9

Currency and Coins Photos courtesy of United States Mint, Bureau of Engraving and Houghton Mifflin Harcourt

Printed in the U.S.A.

ISBN   978-0-358-00229-1

8 9 10   0868   28 27 26 25 24 23 22

4500851007   C D E F G

Dear Students and Families,

Welcome to *Into Math, Grade 5!* In this program, you will develop skills and make sense of mathematics by solving real-world problems, using hands-on tools and strategies, and collaborating with your classmates.

With the support of your teacher and by engaging with meaningful practice, you will learn to persevere when solving problems. *Into Math* will not only help you deepen your understanding of mathematics, but also build your confidence as a learner of mathematics.

Even more exciting, you will write all your ideas and solutions right in your book. In your *Into Math* book, writing and drawing on the pages will help you think deeply about what you are learning, help you truly understand math, and most important, you will become a confident user of mathematics!

Sincerely,
The Authors

© Houghton Mifflin Harcourt Publishing Company

Authors

Edward B. Burger, PhD
President, Southwestern University
Georgetown, Texas

Matthew R. Larson, PhD
Past-President, National Council
of Teachers of Mathematics
Lincoln Public Schools
Lincoln, Nebraska

Juli K. Dixon, PhD
Professor, Mathematics Education
University of Central Florida
Orlando, Florida

Steven J. Leinwand
Principal Research Analyst
American Institutes for Research
Washington, DC

Timothy D. Kanold, PhD
Mathematics Educator
Chicago, Illinois

Jennifer Lempp
Educational Consultant
Alexandria, Virginia

Consultants

English Language Development Consultant

Harold Asturias
Director, Center for Mathematics
Excellence and Equity
Lawrence Hall of Science, University of California
Berkeley, California

Program Consultant

David Dockterman, EdD
Lecturer, Harvard Graduate School of Education
Cambridge, Massachusetts

Blended Learning Consultant

Weston Kieschnick
Senior Fellow
International Center for Leadership in Education
Littleton, Colorado

STEM Consultants

Michael A. DiSpezio
Global Educator
North Falmouth, Massachusetts

Marjorie Frank
Science Writer and
Content-Area Reading Specialist
Brooklyn, New York

Bernadine Okoro
Access and Equity and
STEM Learning Advocate and Consultant
Washington, DC

Cary I. Sneider, PhD
Associate Research Professor
Portland State University
Portland, Oregon

Whole Numbers, Expressions, and Volume

(Build Understanding   (Connect Concepts and Skills   (Apply and Practice

MODULE 4 Expressions

○ Build Understanding ○ Connect Concepts and Skills ○ Apply and Practice

MODULE 5 Volume

Unit 2 Add and Subtract Fractions and Mixed Numbers

Build Understanding   Connect Concepts and Skills   Apply and Practice

MODULE 7 Add and Subtract Fractions and Mixed Numbers with Unlike Denominators

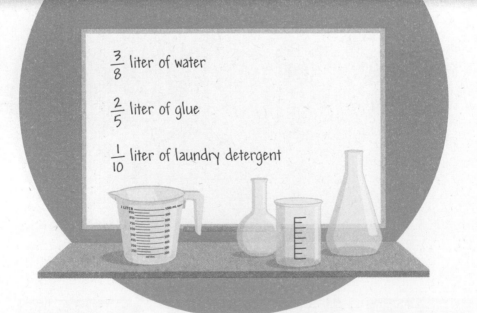

$\frac{3}{8}$ liter of water

$\frac{2}{5}$ liter of glue

$\frac{1}{10}$ liter of laundry detergent

Build Understanding   Connect Concepts and Skills   Apply and Practice

MODULE 9 Understand and Apply Multiplication of Mixed Numbers

Build Understanding   Connect Concepts and Skills   Apply and Practice

Whole Numbers, Expressions, and Volume

Aerospace Engineer

© Houghton Mifflin Harcourt Publishing Company • Image Credit: ©NASA Photo/Alamy

Have you heard the phrase, "This is not rocket science"? Well, for aerospace engineers, what they do certainly IS rocket science! These engineers design rockets that blast into space and airplanes that glide through the sky. They use their advanced mathematical skills to build the machines and test them to make sure they are working safely.

Aerospace engineers are part of a team of people who work together and help each other. One person might do the math calculations. Some work together to make models and others build prototypes and test them.

STEM Task:

Make a straw rocket. Wrap a piece of paper around a marker, tape it, and slide it off. Tape a paper topper to one end. Slip the rocket over a straw. Team up with a partner to test your rockets. Blow the straw to launch the rocket and then measure how far it flies. Work together to modify your designs and test your rockets again. Did they go farther?

Learning Mindset
Strategic Help-Seeking
Identifies Need for Help

How do you know when you need help? When you are stuck, sometimes you can help yourself get unstuck. One way to do this is talking about the problem. Another strategy is to look for tools, like a model, which can help you understand the problem. Or you can try a similar problem that is simpler. But, if you are still stuck, you can also ask for help from others. You may need more help from others in the beginning, but as you practice using the tools to get yourself unstuck, you will get better at helping yourself.

Reflect

Q Were you able to identify if you needed help to construct or operate your rocket? What strategies did you use to help yourself?

Q How did working with a partner help you improve your rocket design? How did it help your partner?

Whole Number Place Value and Multiplication

What is the **value** of that 3?

- Write a term from the box that describes the value of the digit 3 shown by the description of each picture.

tens
hundreds
thousands
hundred thousands

Speed of light (kilometers per second)

3 _____

Minimum age of a U.S. senator (years)

3 _____

Distance from Miami to San Francisco (miles)

San Francisco

Miami

3 _____

Weight of a harbor seal (pounds)

3 _____

Turn and Talk

How can you compare the values of the numbers above?

Are You Ready?

Complete these problems to review prior concepts and skills you will need for this module.

Place Value

Write the digit in its place-value position.

1 4,573

_____ thousands

_____ hundreds

_____ tens

_____ ones

2 3,894

_____ thousands

_____ hundreds

_____ tens

_____ ones

3 6,432

_____ thousands

_____ hundreds

_____ tens

_____ ones

Regroup Through Thousands

Regroup and rename the number.

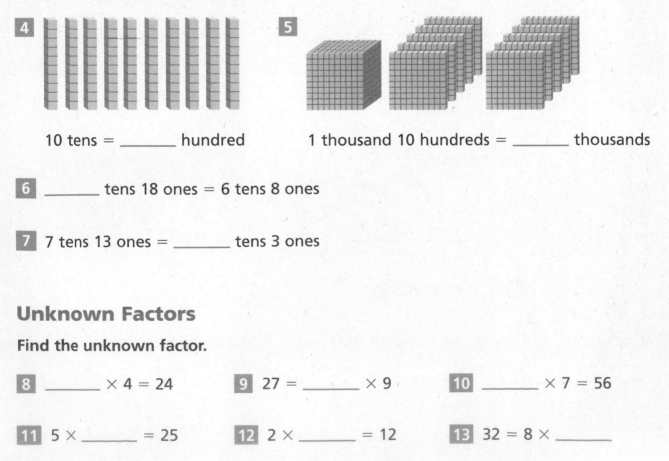

4 10 tens = _____ hundred

5 1 thousand 10 hundreds = _____ thousands

6 _____ tens 18 ones = 6 tens 8 ones

7 7 tens 13 ones = _____ tens 3 ones

Unknown Factors

Find the unknown factor.

8 _____ × 4 = 24

9 27 = _____ × 9

10 _____ × 7 = 56

11 5 × _____ = 25

12 2 × _____ = 12

13 32 = 8 × _____

Name

Recognize the 10 to 1 Relationship Among Place-Value Positions

(I Can) describe place-value relationships in multi-digit whole numbers.

Spark Your Learning

On a road trip, Anna and her family stop at a ranch where bales of hay are being weighed. Describe the relationship between the two weights. How can you use the relationship to compare the weights?

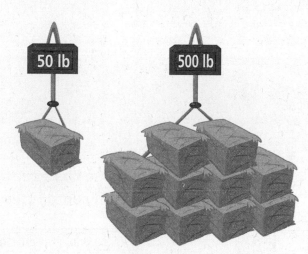

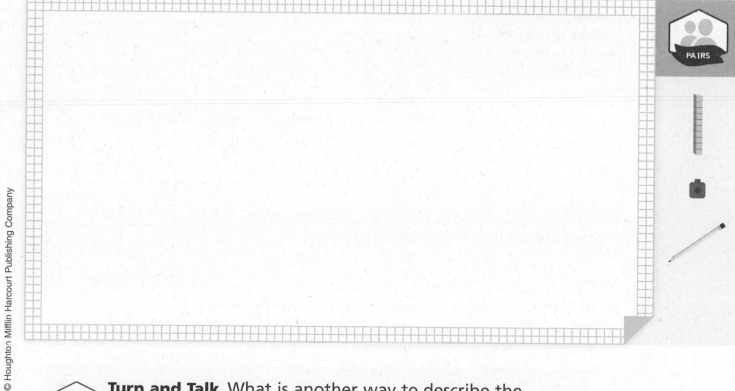

PAIRS

Turn and Talk What is another way to describe the relationship between the weights? How can you use that relationship to compare the weights?

Build Understanding

1 Anna's aunt opens a savings account for her. Anna, her brother, and her aunt all make contributions. The amount of each contribution is shown.

Anna's aunt   Anna's brother   Anna

A. Complete the place-value chart to show the amount of money that each person contributes.

	Thousands	Hundreds	Tens	Ones
Anna's aunt				
Anna's brother				
Anna				

B. What is the relationship between the amount of money Anna's aunt contributes and the amount Anna's brother contributes?

_____

C. How does the position of the digit 2 change when the amount Anna's brother contributes is multiplied by 10?

_____

D. What is the relationship between the amount Anna contributes and the amount Anna's brother contributes?

_____

E. How does the position of the digit 2 change when finding $\frac{1}{10}$ of the amount Anna's brother contributes?

_____

2 **A.** Complete each column in the table.

Number	10 times as much	1 times as much	$\frac{1}{10}$ of
7,000			700
800		800	
600,000	6,000,000		

B. How does the number of zeros in each number change

- in the "10 times as much" column?

  _____

- in the "1 times as much" column?

  _____

- in the "$\frac{1}{10}$ of" column?

  _____

 Turn and Talk Explain how you found the unknown values in each row.

· ·

Check Understanding Math Board

1 There are 60 students on a school bus. One-tenth of the students are in fifth grade. How many fifth graders are there?

_____ of 60 students is _____

2 When 600 is multiplied by 10, how does the position of the digit 6 change?

_____

3 What number is 10 times as much as 200? _____

4 What number is $\frac{1}{10}$ of 900,000? _____

On Your Own

5 (MP) **Use Tools** How do you know that 400 is 10 times as much as 40? Show your work.

_____

6 Use the place-value chart to describe how 800,000 and 8,000,000 compare to each other.

One Millions	Hundred Thousands	Ten Thousands	One Thousands	Hundreds	Tens	Ones

_____

_____

7 What number is 10 times as much as 5,000? _____

8 What number is $\frac{1}{10}$ of 900? _____

9 (MP) **Attend to Precision** Gavin has 30 stickers. Marissa has 300 stickers. Write a sentence that relates the number of stickers Gavin has to the number of stickers Marissa has.

_____

10 **Open Ended** The answer to a place-value question is 50,000. What could be the question?

_____

I'm in a Learning Mindset!

How did using a table help me understand the relationship between two place-value positions?

_____

Name _____

Use Powers of 10 and Exponents

(I Can) rewrite expressions involving the product of a one-digit number and a power of 10 as a whole number.

Spark Your Learning

A local business has set up a website to raise money for a playground. Each donation is $10. For the first 10 days, the account receives 10 donations each day. How much does the account receive the first day? How much does the account receive after 10 days? Explain your thinking.

SMALL GROUPS

Turn and Talk How can you write each amount using multiplication?

Build Understanding

1 One bag of playground sand is shown. How many cubic inches of sand are in 10 bags?

A. Use multiplication to show the number of cubic inches of sand in 10 bags. How many cubic inches of sand is this?

_____

B. How can you write 1,000 as a product using only factors of 10? Explain how you know.

_____

_____

_____

_____

C. How many factors of 10 are needed to write 1,000 as a product using only factors of 10? How many factors of 10 are needed to write 10,000 as a product using only factors of 10?

_____

D. How can you write the number of cubic inches of sand in 10 bags in exponent form?

_____

E. A power is the number that results from repeatedly multiplying a number by itself. How can you write the answer in Part D in word form?

_____

> **Connect to Vocabulary**
>
> You can represent repeated factors using a base and an exponent. The **base** is the number used as a repeated factor. The **exponent** is the number that shows how many times the base is used as a factor.
>
> $$\underset{\text{3 factors}}{10 \times 10 \times 10} = \underset{\text{base}}{10}^{\overset{\text{exponent}}{3}} = 1,000$$
>
> **Exponent form:** 10^3
> **Word form:** the third power of ten

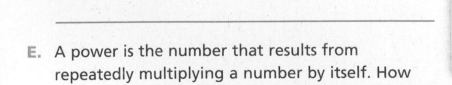

Turn and Talk For powers of 10, 10^1 means one factor of 10, or 1×10. 10^2 means two factors of 10, or $1 \times 10 \times 10$. What do you think 10^0 means?

Step It Out

2 A company sells 10^6 cell phones per week for 7 weeks. The total number of cell phones sold is 7×10^6 phones. How many phones is this, written as a whole number?

A. Write 7×10^0, 7×10^1, 7×10^2, 7×10^3, 7×10^4, 7×10^5, and 7×10^6 as whole numbers.

$7 \times 10^0 = 7 \times 1 = $ _____

$7 \times 10^1 = 7 \times 10 = $ _____

$7 \times 10^2 = 7 \times 10 \times 10 = $ _____

$7 \times 10^3 = 7 \times 10 \times 10 \times 10 = $ _____

$7 \times 10^4 = 7 \times 10 \times 10 \times 10 \times 10 = $ _____

$7 \times 10^5 = 7 \times 10 \times 10 \times 10 \times 10 \times 10 = $ _____

$7 \times 10^6 = 7 \times 10 \times 10 \times 10 \times 10 \times 10 \times 10 = $ _____

B. How many phones are sold in seven weeks? _____

Turn and Talk What pattern do you see between the number of zeros in the product and the exponent?

Check Understanding [Math Board]

1 The attendance at a music festival is 100,000 people. Write the number in exponent form and in word form.

Exponent form: _____

Word form: _____

Multiply.

2 3×10^4

3 7×10^2

4 8×10^5

_____   _____   _____

On Your Own

5 The population of a city is 1,000,000. Write the number in exponent form and in word form.

Exponent form: _____

Word form: _____

Multiply.

6 1×10^2

_____

7 5×10^3

_____

8 2×10^4

_____

9 (MP) **Attend to Precision** What is the value of n in $10^4 = 10 \times 10^n$?

- $10^4 = 10 \times$ _____ $\times$ _____ $\times$ _____

- $10^4 = 10 \times$ _____

The value of n is _____.

10 (MP) **Use Repeated Reasoning** How can you use patterns in the number of zeros to find the value of the unknown exponent in $9 \times 10^{\blacksquare} = 900,000$?

_____

_____

11 (MP) **Attend to Precision** The local business raised 8×10^2 dollars after 8 days and 1×10^3 dollars after 10 days. How much was raised during the last two days? Write your answer using exponents. Show your work.

_____

➗ I'm in a Learning Mindset!

What is still unclear about powers of 10 and exponents?

_____

Name _____

Use a Pattern to Multiply by Multiples of 10, 100, and 1,000

(**I Can**) use mental math to find the product of any two numbers that have one nonzero digit and are multiples of 10, 100, or 1,000.

Step It Out

1 Sixty students participate in a jump-a-thon, and each student jumps rope 400 times. What is the total number of jumps?

A. What multiplication equation models the total number of jumps?

_____

B. Complete the multiplication fact.

$6 \times 4 =$ _____

C. Use the fact to complete the pattern.

$6 \times 40 = (6 \times 4) \times 10^1 =$ _____

$6 \times 400 = (6 \times 4) \times 10^2 =$ _____

$60 \times 400 = (6 \times 10) \times (4 \times 10^2)$

$= (6 \times 4) \times (10 \times 10^2)$

$= (6 \times 4) \times 10^3$

$=$ _____

D. What is the total number of jumps? _____

 Turn and Talk What is the relationship between the number of zeros in the two factors and the number of zeros in the product?

Step It Out

2 Fifty students each jump rope 2,000 times during the jump-a-thon.

A. What multiplication equation models the number of jumps completed by the 50 students?

_____

B. Complete the multiplication fact and the pattern.

$5 \times 2 =$ _____

$5 \times 20 = (5 \times 2) \times 10^1 =$ _____

$5 \times 200 = (5 \times 2) \times 10^2 =$ _____

$5 \times 2{,}000 = (5 \times 2) \times 10^3 =$ _____

$50 \times 2{,}000 = (5 \times 10) \times (2 \times 10^3)$

$\qquad\qquad = (5 \times 2) \times (10 \times 10^3)$

$\qquad\qquad = (5 \times 2) \times 10^4$

$\qquad\qquad =$ _____

C. How many jumps were completed by these students? _____

Turn and Talk Why is the total number of zeros in the product not always the same as the total number of zeros in the two factors?

Check Understanding Math Board

1 The 40 students in Leona's grade each did 3,000 jumping jacks.

How many jumping jacks is this? _____

Multiply.

2 $70 \times 600 =$ _____

3 $30 \times 8{,}000 =$ _____

4 _____ $= 80 \times 5{,}000$

5 $50 \times 600 =$ _____

On Your Own

Complete the multiplication fact and pattern.

6 $6 \times 9 = $ _____

$(6 \times 9) \times 10^1 = $ _____

$(6 \times 9) \times 10^2 = $ _____

$(6 \times 9) \times 10^3 = $ _____

7 $3 \times 8 = $ _____

$(3 \times 8) \times 10^1 = $ _____

$(3 \times 8) \times 10^2 = $ _____

$(3 \times 8) \times 10^3 = $ _____

8 $5 \times 4 = $ _____

$(5 \times 4) \times 10^1 = $ _____

$(5 \times 4) \times 10^2 = $ _____

$(5 \times 4) \times 10^3 = $ _____

$(5 \times 4) \times 10^4 = $ _____

9 $12 \times 8 = $ _____

$(12 \times 8) \times 10^1 = $ _____

$(12 \times 8) \times 10^2 = $ _____

$(12 \times 8) \times 10^3 = $ _____

$(12 \times 8) \times 10^4 = $ _____

Find the unknown number.

10 $40 \times 70{,}000 = 28 \times 10^{\blacksquare}$

_____

11 $60 \times 5{,}000 = 3 \times 10^{\blacksquare}$

_____

12 $30 \times \blacksquare = 21 \times 10^6$

_____

13 $50 \times \blacksquare = 2 \times 10^4$

_____

Multiply.

14 $80 \times 400 = $ _____

15 $50 \times 200 = $ _____

16 $30 \times 7{,}000 = $ _____

17 $40 \times 5{,}000 = $ _____

18 A shipping company buys 60 trucks for $30,000 each.

What is the total cost? _____

19 What is the total weight of 20 similar semi-truck

cabs and trailers? _____

30,000 lb

20 Thirty other students participate in the jump-a-thon, and they each jump rope 600 times. What is the total number of jumps?

_____

21 Four hundred students each jump rope 70 times. What is the total number of jumps for this group of students?

_____

22 (MP) **Use Repeated Reasoning** A store sells 50 basketball backboards and stands for $700 each. How much does the store earn from these sales? Use a multiplication fact and a pattern.

How much does the store earn? _____

23 (MP) **Use Structure** How many zeros are in the product of any nonzero whole number and 1,000? Explain your answer.

_____

_____

_____

24 (MP) **Use Repeated Reasoning** What is $(3 \times 10^2) \times (9 \times 10^3)$? Use a multiplication fact and a pattern.

What is the product? _____

Name _____

Multiply by 1-Digit Numbers

(I Can) **multiply multi-digit whole numbers by 1-digit numbers using regrouping and place value.**

Step It Out

1 Adah walks 1,274 steps once around her neighborhood. If she walks around her neighborhood 3 times, how many steps does she walk?

A. Estimate the number of steps Adah walks. Show your work.

_____

_____

B. Multiply to find the number of steps she walks.

- Multiply the ones.

  Regroup _____ ones as _____.

- Multiply the tens. Add the regrouped tens.

  _____ tens + _____ ten = _____ tens

- Multiply the hundreds. Add the regrouped hundreds.

  _____ hundreds + _____ hundreds = _____ hundreds

- Multiply the thousands.

  Adah walks _____ steps.

$$
\begin{array}{r}
\square\ \ \square \\
1,\ \ 2\ \ 7\ \ 4 \\
\times\ \ \ \ \ \ \ \ \ \ 3 \\
\hline
\square,\square\square\square
\end{array}
$$

C. How do you know if your answer is reasonable?

_____

_____

 Turn and Talk In multiplying 1,274 by 5, what does recording 3 above the digit 2 represent?

Step It Out

2 Michael walks to and from school each day. The round-trip distance is 4,206 feet. What is the total distance he walks to and from school in 5 days?

A. Estimate the total distance. Show your work.

_____

B. Jason's solution is shown. Work through the steps to solve the problem, and then determine his error.

- Multiply the ones.

- Multiply the tens.

- Complete the problem.

- What is the total distance? _____

```
    1 3
   4,206
 ×     5
 ──────
  21,300
```

☐   ☐
4, 2 0 6
×   5
┌──┬──┬──┬──┬──┐
│ │ │, │ │ │
└──┴──┴──┴──┴──┘

C. Compare your work with Jason's. What error did Jason make?

_____

• •

Check Understanding **Math Board**

Estimate. Then find the product.

1 Estimate: _____

```
   868
 ×   4
```

2 Estimate: _____

```
  4,805
 ×    8
```

3 Estimate: _____

```
  9,372
 ×    7
```

4 A kilometer is approximately 1,094 yards. Toby runs a 6-kilometer race. About how many yards does he run?

_____

18

On Your Own

Estimate. Then find the product.

5 Estimate: _____

    915
×   3
___

6 Estimate: _____

   1,352
×   9
___

7 Estimate: _____

  4,306
×   4
___

8 Estimate: _____

  5,033
×   7
___

9 Estimate: _____

  8,926
×   5
___

10 Estimate: _____

  27,158
×   6
___

Find the unknown digits.

11
    4 3 8
×   7
_____
3, ☐ 6 6

12
  4, 9 3 ☐
×   3
_____
1 ☐, 8 ☐ 7

13
  5, ☐ 3 4
×   9
_____
4 ☐, 8 ☐ ☐

14 In Michael's neighborhood, there is a rectangular pathway that is 152 feet long and 9 feet wide. What is the area of the pathway?

_____

15 A farmer has a corn field with 9 rows of corn. Each row has 1,026 corn plants. How many corn plants are there?

_____

16 Martha runs 1,760 yards each day for 3 days. How many yards does she run?

_____

On Your Own

17 **Health and Fitness** Darlene walks around her neighborhood. Her daily goal is to walk 4,000 steps.

852 steps

- Does Darlene reach her daily goal if she walks around her neighborhood 5 times? Make an estimate to answer the question and show your work.

_____

_____

- How many steps does Darlene take if she walks around her neighborhood 5 times? Show your work.

_____

18 **(MP) Reason** Marisha solves a multiplication problem but leaves out some of her work. What are the unknown values of *a* and *b*? Explain how you know by describing place values and regrouping.

$$
\begin{array}{r}
\ ^{a}\ \ ^{b} \\
5,912 \\
\times7 \\
\hline
41,384
\end{array}
$$

_____

_____

_____

_____

19 **(MP) Critique Reasoning** Francisco solves a multiplication problem but makes an error.

$$
\begin{array}{r}
^{2}\ \ ^{4} \\
4,315 \\
\times8 \\
\hline
34,420
\end{array}
$$

- What error does he make and what is the correct answer?

_____

_____

Name _____

Multiply by Multi-Digit Numbers

(**I Can**) multiply multi-digit whole numbers by 2-digit or 3-digit numbers.

Step It Out

1 The cost for a summer camp is $1,125 for each camper. If 65 campers sign up, what is the total amount the camp collects?

A. Estimate 65 × 1,125. Show your work.

_____

B. Multiply by the ones. Then record.

5 ones × 1,125 = _____ ones

C. Multiply by the tens. Think about how you regroup. Then record.

6 tens × 1,125 = _____ tens

or _____ ones

D. Add the partial products.

E. What is the total amount the camp collects? _____

F. Is the answer reasonable? Explain.

_____

_____

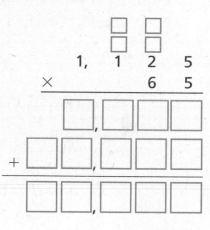

 Turn and Talk Will there always be a 0 in the ones column of the second partial product when multiplying by a two-digit number? Explain.

© Houghton Mifflin Harcourt Publishing Company

Step It Out

2 An online store sells camping chairs for $29. If the store sells 26,578 chairs in one year, how much does the store earn in sales?

A. Estimate 26,578 × 29. Show your work.

_____

B. Multiply by the ones and record.

9 ones × 26,578 = _____ ones

C. Multiply by the tens and record. Think about how you regroup.

2 tens × 26,578 = _____ tens

or _____ ones

D. Add the partial products and record.

E. How much does the store earn? _____

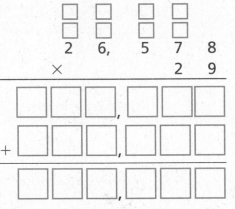

 Turn and Talk How would the partial products change if you were to multiply by a 3-digit number instead of a 2-digit number?

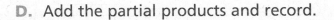

Check Understanding Math Board

1 The camp director says that there should be 28 bottles of water for each camper. If the camp expects to have 564 campers during the summer, how many bottles of water should the camp have?

_____

Estimate. Then find the product.

2 813 × 76   **3** 4,359 × 45   **4** 31,289 × 52

On Your Own

Estimate. Then find the product.

5 Estimate: _____

379
× 28

6 Estimate: _____

654
× 97

7 Estimate: _____

8,292
× 76

8 Estimate: _____

24,736
× 93

9 Estimate: _____

56,374
× 32

10 Estimate: _____

5,341
× 105

11 **STEM** A distant star is 2,760 light years from Earth. The Large Magellanic Cloud is 59 times as many light years from Earth. How many light years from Earth is the Large Magellanic Cloud? How do you know whether your answer is reasonable?

_____

_____

_____

_____

_____

12 A commuter plane flies the same route 24 times in one week. The route is 1,384 miles. How many miles does the plane fly in one week?

_____

On Your Own

13 **Financial Literacy** Each unit in a new building sells for $86,650. There are 32 units available. Estimate and then find how much is earned if all 32 units are sold.

_____

14 (MP) **Use Structure** Complete the place-value chart to find the product of 48 and 7,326. The sum of the products in the table is equal to 48 × 7,326. How is this related to using the standard algorithm for multiplication?

	Thousands	Hundreds	Tens	Ones
	7,000	300	20	6

× 8				
× 40				

_____

_____

15 (MP) **Reason** Find the values for *a*, *b*, and *c* in the multiplication problem.

```
    c 2
    2 a
    5 3 7
  ×   4 6
    3, 2 2 2
+ 2 1, 4 8 b
  2 4, 7 0 2
```

$a = $ _____

$b = $ _____

$c = $ _____

16 **Open Ended** Describe another method you can use to multiply 358 and 45.

_____

_____

Name

Develop Multiplication Fluency

(I Can) set up and solve multistep problems with at least 2 steps.

Step It Out

1 Fun Park Amusement rents food carts, game booths, equipment, and rides for parties, fundraisers, and county fairs. The rental prices are shown in the table.

Attraction	Food Cart	Game Booth	Equipment	Ride
Rental Fee	$59	$79	$99	$149

In May, 36 game booths and 14 rides were rented from Fun Park. How much did Fun Park earn from the game booth and ride rentals in May?

A. What do you need to find?

_____

B. Write a multiplication equation to model each cost.

_____

C. Find each cost. Show your work.

_____

D. How much did Fun Park earn from the game booth and ride rentals in May? Explain how you found the answer.

_____

 Turn and Talk Describe two ways to find how much Fun Park should receive from rentals if the number of game booths rented and the number of rides rented each double in June.

Step It Out

2 New floor tiles are being installed in a restaurant at an amusement park. There are 254 tiles needed to cover the floor. What is the area of the floor?

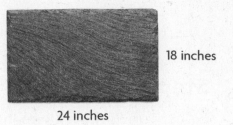

18 inches

24 inches

A. How can you use the measurements of a floor tile to find the area of the restaurant floor?

_____

B. What is the area of each floor tile? Show your work.

C. What is the area of the restaurant floor? Show your work.

_____   _____

Check Understanding 🔲 Math Board

1 This year, a company spends $660 to train one new employee. In 10 years, training costs will be twice that amount. The company expects to hire 635 new employees in the 10th year. How much will the company

spend for training? _____

Use the table showing Fun Park Amusement rental prices for 2 and 3.

Attraction	Food Cart	Game Booth	Equipment	Ride
Rental Fee	$59	$79	$99	$149

2 How much more is the cost to rent 18 rides than to rent 26 game booths?

3 What is the cost to rent 39 food carts and 78 game booths?

_____   _____

26

On Your Own

4 **(MP)** **Model with Mathematics** Cora hits the bullseye (the 75-point circle) 19 times during archery season. She hits the 33-point circle 238 times. What is the total number of points for those hits? Write an equation to model the situation.

_____

5 Shannon burns 46 calories each hour while sleeping. When she plays basketball, she burns 11 times as many calories as she does when sleeping. She burns twice as many calories each hour when she runs than when she plays basketball. How many calories does Shannon burn when she runs for 1 hour?

_____

6 Professional soccer fields measure 105 meters by 68 meters. All 24 teams in a professional league use a special sod for their fields. How much of this special sod is needed for all 24 fields?

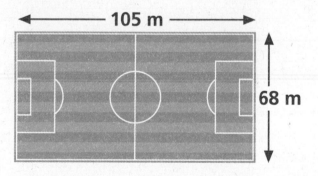

_____

7 Admission tickets to an amusement park cost $18 each. For a class field trip, the park offers a $5 discount on each ticket. How much will tickets cost for 136 students?

_____

8 A company makes hardwood for basketball courts. A basketball court is 94 feet long and 50 feet wide. How much hardwood does the company need to make 12 new courts?

_____

On Your Own

Use the table for 9–12. The table shows the prices of various items at an office supply store.

Item	Desk	Chair	Filing Cabinet	Table
Price	$239	$93	$87	$349

9 If the store sells 35 filing cabinets and 14 tables, how much does it earn? _____

10 Suppose the store sells 12 desks and 9 tables. For which item does the store earn more in sales? How much more does the store earn for this item? _____

11 (MP) **Attend to Precision** A company purchases 16 pairs of desks and chairs. What is the total cost? Describe two ways to find the total cost.

_____

_____

_____

12 (MP) **Critique Reasoning** A company orders 12 filing cabinets. The next day it triples the order. Alyssa and Mario each calculate the total cost of the final order. Who calculated the total cost correctly? Explain your answer.

Alyssa's Work	**Mario's Work**
$\begin{array}{r} 87 \\ \times\ 12 \\ \hline 164 \\ +\ 870 \\ \hline 1{,}034 \end{array}$	$\begin{array}{r} 87 \\ \times\ 12 \\ \hline 174 \\ +\ 87 \\ \hline 261 \end{array}$
$3 \times 1{,}034 = \$3{,}102$	$3 \times 261 = \$783$

_____

_____

Review

Vocabulary

1 Draw lines to match the word to the definition.

base •   • the result of multiplying two or
                                  more numbers

exponent •   • a number used as a repeated
                                  factor

product •   • a number that shows how many times
                                  the base is used as a factor

Concepts and Skills

2 In which number is the place value of the digit 9 ten times
as much as the place value of the digit 9 in 410,917?

(A) 159,230

(B) 305,942

(C) 432,691

(D) 590,231

3 (MP) **Use Tools** Select all the equations that represent a product
of 54,000. Tell what strategy or tool you will use, explain your
choice, and then find the answers.

(A) $2{,}700 \times 2 = \blacksquare$ (D) $54 \times 10^4 = \blacksquare$

(B) $600 \times 90 = \blacksquare$ (E) $9 \times 6 \times 10^3 = \blacksquare$

(C) $1{,}800 \times 30 = \blacksquare$ (F) $(6 \times 10) \times (9 \times 100) = \blacksquare$

_____

_____

4 What number is $\frac{1}{10}$ of 5,000? _____

5 What number is 10 times as much as 40,000? _____

Find the unknown exponent.

6 $4 \times 10^{\blacksquare} = 4{,}000$

7 $7 \times 10^{\blacksquare} = 700{,}000$

_____

_____

Multiply.

8 $67 \times 10^4 = $ _____

9 $160 \times 10^2 = $ _____

10 _____ $= 500 \times 600$

11 _____ $= 90 \times 30{,}000$

12
$$\begin{array}{r} 187 \\ \times\ \ 4 \\ \hline \end{array}$$

13
$$\begin{array}{r} 3{,}160 \\ \times\ \ \ \ 8 \\ \hline \end{array}$$

14
$$\begin{array}{r} 24{,}079 \\ \times\ \ \ \ \ 5 \\ \hline \end{array}$$

15
$$\begin{array}{r} 528 \\ \times\ 73 \\ \hline \end{array}$$

16
$$\begin{array}{r} 17{,}438 \\ \times\ \ \ \ 26 \\ \hline \end{array}$$

17
$$\begin{array}{r} 8{,}023 \\ \times\ \ \ 69 \\ \hline \end{array}$$

18 The planet Neptune takes about 165 years to make a complete orbit around the Sun. About how many years does Neptune take to make 18 complete orbits?

_____

19 Forty boxes of baseballs weigh a total of 1,200 pounds. How many pounds would 4 boxes of baseballs weigh? How many pounds would 400 boxes of baseballs weigh?

_____

20 The population of the town Val lives in is about 8×10^3. The population of the town Vic lives in is about 6×10^4. Whose town has the greater population? By how many people?

_____

Understand Division of Whole Numbers

HOW MANY PEOPLE DOES IT TAKE?

- Imagine a tower of people standing on each other's shoulders.

- Use this information to find the number of people you would need to reach the height of the Burj Khalifa building in Dubai.

- The height of the Burj Khalifa building is about 2,722 feet.

- The distance from a person's feet to their shoulders is about 4 feet.

- The person on top of the tower is 6 feet tall.

- How many people would you need to reach the height of the Burj Khalifa building in Dubai?

_____

 Turn and Talk

- How did you solve the problem?

- How does your answer change if the people are able to balance on each other's heads? (Assume all of the people are 6 feet tall.)

Are You Ready?

Complete these problems to review prior concepts and skills you will need for this module.

Represent Division

Complete the table. Use counters to help.

	Counters	Number of Equal Groups	Number in Each Group
1	21	3	
2	12		2
3	15	5	
4	32		4

Multiples

Write the first six nonzero multiples.

5 4 _____

6 7 _____

7 10 _____

8 8 _____

Subtract Through 4-Digit Numbers: Subtract Across Zeros

Find the difference.

9
$$704$$
$$- 86$$

10
$$800$$
$$- 215$$

11
$$6,501$$
$$- 754$$

12
$$3,002$$
$$- 75$$

13
$$1,032$$
$$- 956$$

14
$$2,308$$
$$- 1,659$$

Name _____

Relate Multiplication to Division

(**I Can**) use an array or an area model to solve a division problem.

PLAYLIST
1 Playground Patter
2 Clean My Room Blues
3 My Blue Bike
4 Rolling On
5 Love My Pet
6 My Comfy Pillow

Spark Your Learning

A community center has 7 digital music players. Each music player has the same number of songs. If there is a total of 112 songs, how many songs are on each music player?

Show your thinking.

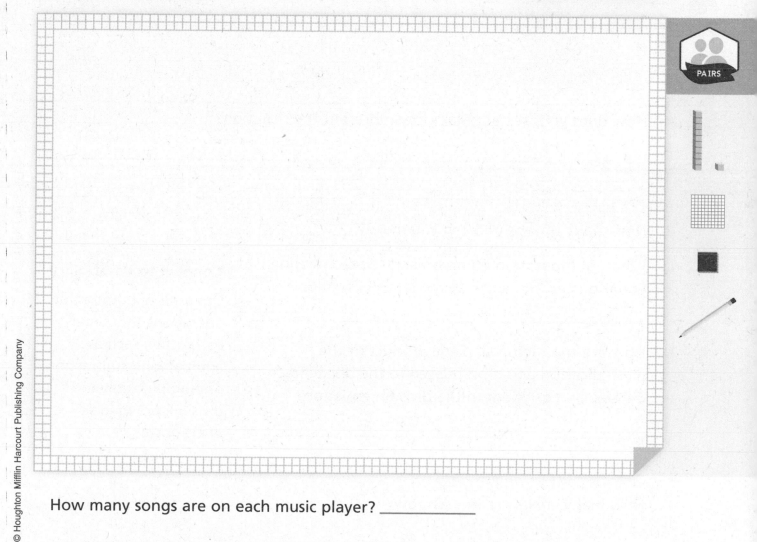

PAIRS

How many songs are on each music player? _____

Turn and Talk How does your answer change if the number of digital music players is 8?

Build Understanding

1 A local theater group is performing a musical. The members arrange 105 chairs in 5 equal rows for the audience. How many chairs are in each row?

Draw a rectangular array to represent the situation.

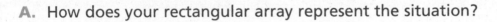

A. How does your rectangular array represent the situation?

_____

_____

B. How many groups of 5 can you make? _____

C. What multiplication equation and related division equation can you write to model the situation?

_____

D. How are the factors and the product of the multiplication equation related to the **dividend**, **divisor**, and **quotient** in the division equation?

_____

_____

E. How many chairs are in each row? _____

 Turn and Talk Why can you use the relationship between multiplication and division to solve a division problem?

© Houghton Mifflin Harcourt Publishing Company • Image Credit: ©Houghton Mifflin Harcourt

2 Simone wants 6 of her friends to share 84 photos equally. How many photos will each friend get?

A. What division and multiplication equations

   model the situation? _____

You can use an area model or the Distributive Property.

B. What are two multiples of 6 that have a sum of 84? Use your multiples to complete the area model.

C. In Part B, how does each smaller rectangle show a quotient and a product?

_____

_____

D. How can you use the quotients of the smaller rectangles

   to find the quotient 84 ÷ 6? _____

E. Use the Distributive Property to show the partial products shown in your area model.

$6 \times \blacksquare = 84$

_____ + _____ = 84

$(6 \times$ _____ $) + (6 \times$ _____ $) = 84$

_____ $\times ($ _____ $+$ _____ $) =$ _____

_____ $\times$ _____ $=$ _____

F. What related division equation can you write to model the number of photos each friend will get?

_____

• •

Check Understanding Math Board

1 Priya and her friends are decorating picture frames. Priya shares 96 beads equally between herself and her 3 friends. How many beads does each of them receive?

Show your work. _____

On Your Own

2 (MP) **Model with Mathematics** Four people make a playlist of 76 songs for a party. Each person provides the same number of songs for the playlist. How many songs does each person provide?

- Draw to represent the situation.

- Write a multiplication equation and a division equation to model the situation. _____

- How many songs does each person provide? _____

3 (MP) **Attend to Precision** Nine friends collect 1,260 leaves at the forest preserve. They each collect the same number of leaves. Explain how to use an equation to find the number of leaves each friend collects.

_____

_____

_____

4 **Open Ended** Write a division word problem that relates to the multiplication equation $9 \times 13 = 117$.

_____

_____

_____

© Houghton Mifflin Harcourt Publishing Company

I'm in a Learning Mindset!

How did I collaborate with a partner when relating multiplication to division?

_____

Name _____

Represent Division with 2-Digit Divisors

(I Can) find the quotient of numbers up to four digits divided by 2-digit divisors using visual models.

Spark Your Learning

You are a game designer designing a treasure hunt game similar to the one shown. The game board is a grid with a treasure chest located behind one of the squares.

The rectangular grid will have 96 squares. If the length of the grid is greater than 10 squares, how wide can the grid be?

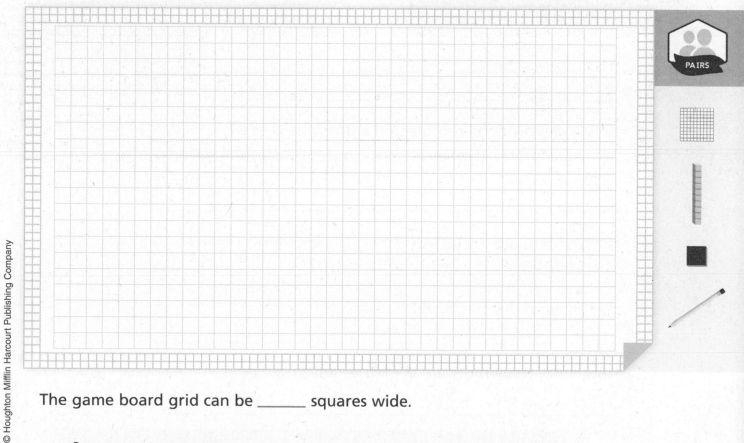

The game board grid can be _____ squares wide.

Turn and Talk Compare your game board grid to the game board grids of other classmates. How do they compare?

Build Understanding

1 You are designing another game in which the player needs
to arrange flowerpots in 12 equal-sized groups. There are
156 flowerpots. How many flowerpots are in each group?

A. What multiplication and division equations can you write
to model the number of flowerpots, *p*, in each group?

_____

B. How can you break apart 156 into a sum of multiples
of 12? Use your multiples to make an area model.

_____

C. What do the number of rows and the number
of columns in the area model represent?

_____

_____

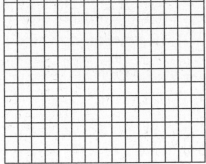

D. How is the dividend represented in the area model?

_____

_____

E. How is the quotient represented in the area model? What
is the quotient?

_____

_____

F. How many flowerpots are in each group?

_____

 Turn and Talk How can you use your equations to explain
how to find the number of flowerpots in each group?

2 There are 675 gold bars hidden throughout the game. The same number of bars are placed in each of 25 treasure chests. How many bars are in each treasure chest?

A. What division equation models this situation?

_____

B. Break apart the dividend into multiples of the divisor and use the area model to find the quotient.

```

                                                  
```

C. Explain what the smaller rectangles represent in terms of the division equation.

_____

_____

_____

D. How many gold bars are in each treasure chest?

_____

 Turn and Talk Compare your area model to the area models of other classmates. What can you conclude?

Build Understanding

3 Archaeologists find a sunken chest of 3,420 bronze coins. If the coins are to be shared equally among 20 museums, how many coins does each museum get?

   A. How can you model this situation using a division equation?

   _____

   B. Draw an area model to find the quotient. How can using a greater multiple of the divisor help you draw the area model?

   _____

   C. How many coins does each museum get? How does your area model show this?

   _____

   _____

Check Understanding [Math Board]

1 There are 76 bottles of paint in the art studio. The art teacher divides them equally among all 19 students in the class. How many bottles of paint does each student get?

   _____

On Your Own

2 (MP) **Model with Mathematics** Lucinda has
81 tulip bulbs. She plants 3 bulbs in each row.
How many rows of tulip bulbs does she plant?
Write a division equation to model this
situation.

_____

3 (MP) **Model with Mathematics** Write a division equation that
is related to the application of the Distributive Property shown.

$12 \times (100 + 20 + 4) = (12 \times 100) + (12 \times 20) + (12 \times 4)$

$= 1,200 + 240 + 48$

$= 1,488$

_____

4 Miguel volunteers at the library. He needs to arrange
576 books on shelves for a book sale. There are 16 empty
shelves. Miguel puts an equal number of books on each shelf.

How many books does he put on each shelf? _____

5 (MP) **Model with Mathematics** Multiplication of two numbers
results in the partial products 200, 10, and 3. One of the factors
is 30. Write a multiplication equation and a division equation to
model this situation. Show your thinking.

6 **STEM** There are 455 grams of dissolved salt in a 13-kilogram
sample of seawater. How many grams of dissolved salt are in

1 kilogram of seawater? _____

On Your Own

(MP) **Use Tools** Use an area model to represent the division equation and find the quotient.

7 $925 \div 25 = c$

_____

8 $q = 2{,}750 \div 10$

_____

9 $t = 1{,}134 \div 54$

_____

10 $672 \div 24 = g$

_____

11 **(MP)** **Model with Mathematics** The area of the bottom of a swimming pool is 1,250 square meters. The length of the pool is 50 meters. What is the width of the swimming pool? Write a division equation to model this situation.

_____

I'm in a Learning Mindset!

What part of representing division of 2-digit divisors am I comfortable solving on my own?

_____

Name

Estimate with 2-Digit Divisors

(I Can) estimate quotients of division problems using
compatible numbers.

Spark Your Learning

One of Florida's tallest buildings is
900 Biscayne Bay. It stands 650 feet
tall. The building has 63 floors. If each
floor is approximately the same height,
about how tall is one floor of the
900 Biscayne Bay building?

Show your thinking.

One floor is about _____ feet tall.

 Turn and Talk How was the strategy you used to estimate
similar to and different from estimating the product of
two factors?

Build Understanding

1 The Icon Brickell South Tower in Miami is 586 feet tall and has about 60 floors. About how many feet high is each floor?

A. Write an equation to model the situation. _____

B. Does the problem require you to find the exact quotient? Explain.

_____

_____

C. What is true about dividends that are compatible with a divisor of 60?

_____

D. What two multiples of 60 are closest to 586?

_____

E. What are two estimates? Show your work.

_____

F. How does each estimate compare to the actual quotient? Explain.

_____

_____

G. Which estimate is closer to the actual quotient? Explain.

_____

H. About how many feet high is each floor?

_____

 Turn and Talk Why would you want to use compatible numbers to find two estimates for the quotient?

> ### Connect to Vocabulary
>
> Previously, you have used mental math to compute and estimate products and quotients. **Compatible numbers** are numbers that are easy to compute with mentally.

Step It Out

2 Kadeem needs to travel to Florida for his job. The cost of the trip for 28 days is $2,475. About how much will this trip cost Kadeem each day?

A. Model the problem with an equation. Are you asked to find an estimate or an exact answer?

_____

B. Sometimes you might have to change both the dividend and the divisor to make numbers that are compatible.

- To what number might you change 28? _____

- Based on your answer, to what numbers might you change

  2,475 to find two different estimates? _____

- How did you choose the numbers? _____

  _____

  _____

C. Use basic facts and patterns to estimate the quotients.

D. About how much will the trip cost Kadeem each day?

_____

Check Understanding [Math Board]

1 Every year, individuals race to the top of U.S. Bank Tower in Los Angeles. The tower has 1,679 steps. A racer reaches the top in 16 minutes. About how many steps does the racer complete in one minute? _____

On Your Own

2 There are 138 ounces of trail mix in a bag. You want to divide the trail mix equally among 18 smaller bags. What is a reasonable estimate for the number of ounces of trail mix that will go into

each smaller bag? _____

3 (MP) **Construct Arguments** Melinda needs to travel for work. A 21-day trip costs $3,750. She says that means the trip will cost about $200 per day. Is her estimate reasonable? Explain.

_____

_____

_____

4 Most Americans spend about 293 hours driving each year. There are 12 months in a year. What is a reasonable estimate for the

number of hours most Americans drive each month? _____

Use compatible numbers to find two estimates.

5 $591 \div 70$

_____

_____

6 $2{,}518 \div 32$

_____

_____

7 **Open Ended** Division of a number by a two-digit number results in a reasonable estimate of 40. Write a division equation

that would result in such an estimate. _____

⬡ I'm in a Learning Mindset!

What types of decisions did I make when estimating quotients of 2-digit divisors?

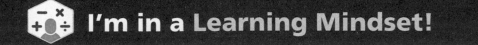

_____

Name

Use Partial Quotients

(I Can) use partial quotients to divide a multi-digit number
by a 2-digit divisor.

Spark Your Learning

Team Mud Footers is participating in an
obstacle course marathon. For each
obstacle the team completes,
$99 is added to their prize bank. The
team completes 12 obstacles. If each
member takes home $66, how many
members are on the team?

SMALL GROUPS

There are _____ members on the team.

Turn and Talk Why would there not be a remainder for a
division problem modeling the context of this situation?

Build Understanding

1 Another team adds $594 to their prize bank. If each member takes home $54, how many members are on the team?

A. What equation can you write to model the number of team members that complete the obstacles?

_____

B. About how many team members complete the obstacles? Show your work.

_____

C. Find the number of members that complete the obstacles by dividing. Use partial quotients.

- What number is the divisor and what number is the dividend?

_____

- Use your estimate. What multiple of the divisor can be subtracted from the dividend? What is this multiple?

_____

- Subtract this multiple from the dividend. What multiple of the divisor can be subtracted from the remaining number? What is this multiple?

_____

- Subtract. What is the **remainder**?

_____

D. How many members are on the team?

_____

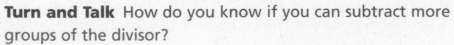 **Turn and Talk** How do you know if you can subtract more groups of the divisor?

Connect to Vocabulary

Sometimes it is easier to divide greater numbers in a few small steps.

Dividing with **partial quotients** means subtracting multiples of the divisor from the dividend until the remaining number is less than the divisor. The partial quotients are then added together to find the whole-number quotient.

Step It Out

2 ▶ A county-wide field day registers 1,468 participants. Each participant receives a ribbon. The ribbons are bundled in packages of 25. How many packages of ribbons are needed?

A. Write a division equation to model the number of packages of ribbons that are needed. What is a reasonable estimate for the number of packages?

_____

B. Divide using partial quotients.

- Subtract multiples of the divisor from the dividend until the remaining number is less than the multiple.

- Subtract smaller multiples of the divisor until the remaining number is less than the divisor.

- Add the partial quotients to find the whole-number quotient.

C. Write the whole-number quotient and remainder.

_____

D. How many packages of ribbons are needed?

_____

• •

Check Understanding 🔲 Math Board

1 There are 439 flower seeds in a packet. A gardener puts 36 seeds in each seed starter tray. How many trays can the gardener fully

fill with one packet of seeds? _____

Divide.

2 728 ÷ 28 _____   **3** 5,836 ÷ 39 _____

On Your Own

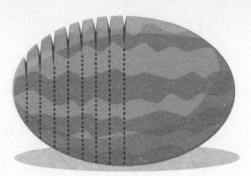

4 There are about 1,932 calories in a 14-pound watermelon. How many calories are there in 1 pound of the watermelon?

_____

5 A third team earns $891 in their prize bank. Each team member receives $81. How many members are on this team?

_____

6 A class of 24 students collects 864 cans for recycling. Each student collects the same number of cans. How many cans does each student collect?

_____

Divide.

7 682 ÷ 31   **8** 2,352 ÷ 48   **9** 7,558 ÷ 62

_____   _____   _____

10 (MP) **Use Repeated Reasoning** Alec and Wanda divide 9,237 by 24 using partial quotients. They both use a multiple of 24 to divide. Alec uses the multiple 480 and Wanda uses the multiple 720. If they each divide correctly, will they both get the same answer? Explain.

_____

_____

⬡ I'm in a Learning Mindset!

How do I break down dividing with 2-digit divisors into smaller steps?

_____

_____

Review

Vocabulary

Choose the correct term from the Vocabulary box.

Vocabulary
compatible numbers
dividend
divisor
partial quotients
quotient
remainder

1 When estimating a quotient, it is best to use

_____ that can be evenly divided.

2 The method of dividing by subtracting multiples of the

divisor from the dividend uses _____.

3 The number that results from dividing is the

_____.

Concepts and Skills

4 Which of the following best describes the division equation represented by the area model?

(A) $190 \div 19 = 10$

(B) $187 \div 17 = 11$

(C) $228 \div 19 = 12$

(D) $238 \div 17 = 14$

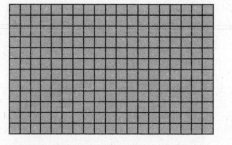

5 (MP) **Use Tools** Select all the division equations for which 50 is a reasonable estimate. Tell what strategy or tool you will use to solve the problem, explain your choice, and then find the answer.

(A) $1{,}386 \div 27 = \blacksquare$ (D) $4{,}193 \div 84 = \blacksquare$

(B) $1{,}164 \div 32 = \blacksquare$ (E) $382 \div 71 = \blacksquare$

(C) $2{,}859 \div 62 = \blacksquare$

6 Write a division equation that is related to the application of the Distributive Property shown.

$$18 \times (200 + 30 + 6) = (18 \times 200) + (18 \times 30) + (18 \times 6)$$
$$= 3{,}600 + 540 + 108$$
$$= 4{,}248$$

_____ ÷ _____ = _____

Use compatible numbers to find two estimates.

7 648 ÷ 44

8 4,174 ÷ 21

_____

_____

_____

_____

9 A local company donates 1,935 ounces of granola to the food bank. Volunteers are making 85 smaller bags. What is a reasonable estimate for the number of ounces of granola in each smaller bag?

_____

Divide.

10 322 ÷ 14

11 591 ÷ 31

12 2,841 ÷ 76

_____

_____

_____

13 1,718 ÷ 23

14 948 ÷ 40

15 4,500 ÷ 84

_____

_____

_____

16 One mile is 5,280 feet long. A certain indoor gym has a running track for which 12 laps around the track is equivalent to 1 mile. Explain how you can use partial quotients to determine how many feet long the track is.

_____

_____

_____

Practice Division of Whole Numbers

What are the unknown digits?

- Each of the digits 1–9 has been removed once from the division problem. Use reasoning to replace those digits.

Use this chart to track your work. Cross off each number as you use it.

1	2	3	4	5	6	7	8	9

$$
\begin{array}{r}
8\ \square\ 8\ r\square \\
\square\overline{)\square,\square\square\square} \\
-\ 4\ 8 \\
\hline
1\ 7 \\
-\ 1\ 2 \\
\hline
\square\ 1 \\
-\ 4\ \square \\
\hline
3
\end{array}
$$

 Turn and Talk

- How do the numbers 48 and 12 help you figure out what the divisor is?

- What else in the structure of the division problem did you use to place numbers?

Are You Ready?

Complete these problems to review prior concepts and skills you will need for this module.

2-Digit Subtraction with Regrouping

Find the difference.

1

Tens	Ones
☐	☐
5	4
− 3	5

2

Tens	Ones
☐	☐
7	2
− 4	8

3

Tens	Ones
☐	☐
8	5
− 6	7

Relate Multiplication and Division

Write the related facts for each set.

4 4, 6, 24

_____ ÷ _____ = _____

_____ × _____ = _____

_____ ÷ _____ = _____

_____ × _____ = _____

5 7, 9, 63

_____ ÷ _____ = _____

_____ × _____ = _____

_____ ÷ _____ = _____

_____ × _____ = _____

6 5, 8, 40

_____ ÷ _____ = _____

_____ × _____ = _____

_____ ÷ _____ = _____

_____ × _____ = _____

Multiply by 1-Digit Numbers

Find the product.

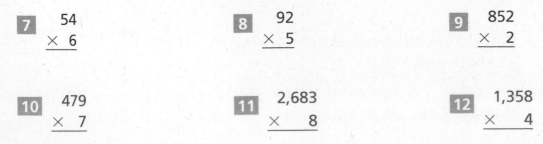

7
```
   54
 ×  6
```

8
```
   92
 ×  5
```

9
```
  852
 ×  2
```

10
```
  479
 ×  7
```

11
```
  2,683
 ×    8
```

12
```
  1,358
 ×    4
```

Name _____

Divide by 2-Digit Divisors

(I Can) use strategies based on place value to divide 3- and 4-digit dividends by 2-digit divisors.

Step It Out

1 Lana makes clothes for her online store. She makes 19 shirts from a large roll of fabric. Each roll has 610 inches of fabric. How many inches of fabric from the roll does Lana use for each shirt?

A. Write a division problem to represent the situation and estimate the answer.

_____

B. Divide the tens. Share the tens equally among the 19 groups.

How many tens are in each group? _____

Multiply the result by the divisor and subtract it from the

dividend. Record. 61 tens − 57 tens = _____ tens

$$19\overline{)610}$$

C. Divide the ones. Regroup 4 tens as 40 ones. Share the ones equally among the 19 groups. How many ones are

in each group? _____

Multiply the result by the divisor and subtract. Record.

40 ones − 38 ones = _____ ones

D. Interpret your answer. Then compare it to your estimate to determine if it is reasonable.

_____

_____

 Turn and Talk What does the remainder tell you about the amount of fabric Lana needs to make another shirt?

Step It Out

2 Lana's shirts are a hit! Fab Fashion is a company with stores across the country as shown. The company orders 1,200 of her shirts. If each store receives the same number of shirts in the first shipment, how many shirts will each store receive?

NOW WITH 38 STORES!

A. Use compatible numbers to estimate 1,200 ÷ 38.

_____

B. Divide the tens. Multiply the result by the divisor and subtract it from the dividend. Record.

$$38\overline{)1{,}200}$$

C. Divide the ones. Multiply the result by the divisor and subtract it from the dividend. Record.

D. How many shirts will each store have, and how many

will be left over? _____

 Turn and Talk Suppose you let *a* represent the dividend, *b* the divisor, *q* the whole-number quotient, and *r* the remainder in a division problem. What equation could you write to show how these values are related? What does the equation model in this situation?

Check Understanding

1 A museum director wants to display 609 objects in 21 rooms so that each room has the same number of objects. Write a division problem to represent the situation. Estimate, and then find, the number of objects to be displayed in each room. Show your division.

_____

On Your Own

2 A conference coordinator has 128 chairs to arrange in 11 rows. If each row has the same number of chairs, how many chairs are in each row? How many chairs are left over?

_____

Divide. Show your work.

3 960 ÷ 24

4 3,279 ÷ 82

_____

_____

5 45)‾7‾6‾9‾

6 39)‾2‾,‾1‾4‾5‾

_____

_____

7 (MP) **Use Repeated Reasoning** A cell phone has 4,515 megabytes of storage space available. Each downloaded song is 12 megabytes, and each downloaded podcast is 84 megabytes.

Space Available:
4,515
Megabytes

- If only songs or only podcasts are downloaded, how many more songs than podcasts can be downloaded? Explain your thinking.

_____

_____

_____

- If the phone is filled with only songs or only podcasts, how many megabytes would be left on the phone?

_____

_____

8 **STEM** Olive is designing a logo for the screen of a video game. The screen is 1,920 pixels wide and 1,080 pixels high. The logo is made up of squares that are each 75 pixels wide and 75 pixels high. How many squares wide and how many squares tall can the logo be?

_____

Divide. Show your work.

9 27)9,099

_____

10 7,293 ÷ 35

_____

11 91)2,763

_____

12 811 ÷ 53

_____

13 (MP) **Use Repeated Reasoning** Krithika makes green dresses with buttons. Each dress requires 11 buttons and 72 inches of green fabric.

- Krithika has a box of 80 buttons and a roll of 500 inches of fabric. How many whole dresses can she make using these items? Explain how you found your answer.

_____

_____

- How many buttons and inches of fabric will be left over after making this number of dresses? How do you know?

_____

Name _____

Interpret the Remainder

(I Can) solve a division problem and interpret the
remainder in the context of the problem.

Step It Out

14 inches

1 A land surveyor rolls a wheeled device on
the ground to measure distances. Each full
turn of the wheel measures 14 inches. The
surveyor measures 1,617 inches of land.
How many turns of the wheel are needed
to measure this distance?

A. Use division to represent the situation.

_____

B. Divide and write the whole-number quotient and

the remainder. _____

C. The remainder indicates that the number of turns
of the wheel is not a whole number. Use the
remainder to find the fractional part of the last turn.

- Write the remainder as the numerator.

- Write the divisor as the denominator.

- What fraction of a turn is represented by the remainder?

_____

D. Write the answer as a whole number of turns and a
fractional part of a turn. How many turns of the wheel are

needed to measure 1,617 inches? _____

Turn and Talk How are the divisor, whole-number quotient,
and remainder used to represent the number of groups and
the size of each group in this situation?

Step It Out

2 A large plot of farmland will be used for a new field. The seed that the farmers will plant on this field is sold in large tanks. Each tank can cover 72 acres with seed. How many tanks are needed to cover the entire field with seed?

Field size: 1,140 acres

A. Represent the situation using a division problem. Identify the dividend and the divisor.

_____

B. Divide to find the whole-number quotient and the remainder. Show your work.

$72\overline{)1,140}$

C. The seed is sold only in full tanks. How many tanks must be purchased to cover the entire field? _____

D. How many acres will the seed from the last tank cover?

_____

 Turn and Talk If this remainder is expressed as a fraction, what information would the fraction give? Explain.

Check Understanding [Math Board]

1 Milo will cut a 136-foot-long roll of wire into 16 equal lengths for fencing. He finds that 136 ÷ 16 is 8 r8. How long will each length of wire measure?

_____

2 Trina has 232 books to put onto shelves. Each shelf can hold 38 books. She plans to fill each shelf before starting the next. She finds that 232 ÷ 38 is 6 r4. How many books will be on each shelf?

_____

On Your Own

3 (MP) **Reason** A vitamin company produces 4,514 tablets every hour. A machine drops the same number of tablets into each bottle. How many bottles does the machine completely fill every hour?

_____

4 (MP) **Reason** To watch a safety video, 294 employees will be arranged into conference rooms that each hold 30 people. The remaining people will watch the video in the cafe. How many people will watch the video in the cafe?

_____

5 (MP) **Attend to Precision** A fabric store orders 2,345 spools of thread. If each shipping box holds 84 spools, how many shipping boxes are needed for this order? Explain your thinking.

_____

_____

_____

Divide. Interpret the remainder to solve.

6 A company ships new basketballs in boxes that fit up to 14 basketballs. How many boxes are needed for an order of 202 basketballs?

7 At a banquet hall, each table requires 18 plates. The kitchen has 387 plates available. How many full tables can be set?

_____

8 A spacecraft collects 234 pounds of rocks from the moon. The rocks are divided evenly among 36 groups of scientists for study. What weight of rocks does each group receive?

9 At the Kennedy Space Center, 138 people are divided into 15 equal groups. The remaining people will form a sixteenth group. How many people will be in the sixteenth group?

_____

On Your Own

10 **Open Ended** Write two word problems that can be represented by using 200 ÷ 12.

- Write a word problem for which the answer is 17.

_____

_____

- Write a word problem for which the answer is 8.

_____

_____

11 Uma brings 600 fluid ounces of lemonade to a picnic. She also brings a package of 48 plastic cups.

- If she fills each cup with the same amount of lemonade,

how much will be in each cup? _____

- Why does it make sense to express this quotient using a fraction?

_____

12 (MP) **Reason** Pulp Paper Company is having a paper airplane design contest. They receive 391 submissions. The judges review the paper airplanes in groups of 16. How many equal groups of paper airplanes will the judges review? How many paper airplanes will be left after the equal groups are judged?

_____

13 (MP) **Construct Arguments** Mr. Torres has 212 coins in his collection. He wants to keep all of his coins in a binder. He can store 24 coins on each binder page. He finds 212 ÷ 24 to be 8 r20, so he buys 8 pages. Does Mr. Torres buy the correct number of pages? Explain.

_____

_____

Name _____

Adjust Quotients

(**I Can**) adjust a digit in a whole-number quotient based on whether an estimate is too low or too high.

Step It Out

1 A ship with scientific equipment is mapping the ocean floor. The equipment can scan 24 square kilometers of ocean floor each day. How many days will the ship take to scan 941 square kilometers?

A. Use compatible numbers to estimate 941 ÷ 24.

_____

B. Use the first digit of your estimate as the first digit of the whole-number quotient. Is your estimate too low, too high, or correct?

$24\overline{)941}$

_____

C. Adjust the first digit based on your results, and then divide.

$24\overline{)941}$

How many tens are left? _____

D. Divide the ones. Estimate the whole-number quotient and use the number. Is your estimate too low, too high, or correct?

_____

E. Adjust the second digit based on your results, and then divide. Interpret the remainder to answer the question.

Since 941 ÷ 24 is _____, it will take the ship _____ days to scan 941 square kilometers.

  Turn and Talk How do you know if your estimate for a digit in the whole-number quotient is too high or too low?

Step It Out

2 A robot submarine is sent to collect fish deep underwater. The mission is to collect at least 2,150 fish. The submarine makes 35 trips and collects the same number of fish on each trip. How many fish does the submarine have to collect during each trip?

A. Use compatible numbers to estimate 2,150 ÷ 35.

_____

B. Use the first digit of your estimate as the first digit of the whole-number quotient. Is your estimate too low, too high,

or correct? _____

C. Adjust the first digit as needed, then divide. How many tens

are left? _____

D. Divide the ones. Estimate the whole-number quotient and use the number. Is your estimate too low, too high, or correct?

_____

E. Adjust the second digit as needed, then divide. Interpret the remainder to answer the question.

Since 2,150 ÷ 35 is _____, the submarine has to collect

_____ fish on each of its trips.

Check Understanding [Math Board]

1 Cindy wants to back up 1,562 computer files by dividing them equally onto 44 thumb drives. She estimates 1,600 ÷ 40 = 40. How does she know that her estimate of 40 tens is too high for

the whole-number quotient? _____

© Houghton Mifflin Harcourt Publishing Company • Image Credit: ©Kip Evans/Alamy

On Your Own

2 (MP) **Attend to Precision** A new theater complex opens and sells 1,296 tickets. The same number of tickets is sold for each of its theaters. To find this number of tickets, the theater owner makes an estimate: 1,200 ÷ 20 = 60. Explain how to find the number of tickets sold for each theater using this estimate.

_____

_____

_____

_____

Describe the estimated digit in the whole-number quotient as _too high_, _too low_, or _correct_. Adjust the estimated digit if needed. Then divide.

3 $81 \overline{)3{,}735}$ with 5 above

4 $63 \overline{)4{,}473}$ with 7 above

5 $97 \overline{)6{,}388}$ with 5 above

_____   _____   _____

6 $45 \overline{)3{,}619}$ with 7 above

7 $28 \overline{)1{,}398}$ with 5 above

8 $79 \overline{)6{,}429}$ with 8 above

_____   _____   _____

9 $32 \overline{)2{,}136}$ with 7 above

10 $53 \overline{)2{,}128}$ with 4 above

11 $64 \overline{)4{,}391}$ with 7 above

_____   _____   _____

Write a division equation that estimates the value of the expression. Then use your estimate to divide, adjusting numbers as needed.

12 1,598 ÷ 34

13 4,398 ÷ 59

14 2,964 ÷ 78

_____   _____   _____

65

On Your Own

15 (MP) **Critique Reasoning** Amanda and Jessica each make a different estimate before dividing 1,305 ÷ 26.

- Amanda's estimate is 1,200 ÷ 30 = 40. How did Amanda adjust the first digit from the estimate to find the first digit in the whole-number quotient?

_____

- Jessica's estimate is 1,200 ÷ 20 = 60. How did Jessica adjust the first digit from the estimate to find the first digit in the whole-number quotient?

_____

16 (MP) **Attend to Precision** A new machine can cut 2,576 blocks each day. This is 28 times as many blocks as the current machine can cut each day. How many blocks can the current machine cut each day? Make an estimate. Then use your estimate to divide.

_____

17 Jaime wants to put 2,936 movie posters into 85 tubes, with the same number in each tube. He finds two estimates for the expression 2,936 ÷ 85: 2,700 ÷ 90 = 30 and 3,200 ÷ 80 = 40.

- Use each estimate to divide. What adjustments, if any, must be made using each estimate?

_____

_____

- What does your work tell you about finding different estimates for the same division expression?

_____

_____

_____

Name _____

Practice with Division

(**I Can**) solve a division problem by using a bar model
or an equation.

Step It Out

1 A comic book store sold 8 times as many
copies of the Team Amazing comic book
as it sold of the Astonishing Force comic
book. The store sold 549 copies of both
comic books. How many copies of each
comic book were sold?

A. Use a bar model to represent the situation. Label the bars
and the total number of copies represented.

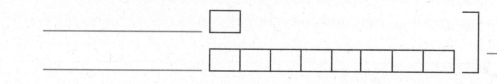

B. Write an equation to find the number represented by each
box of the bar model. Then find the number.

_____

C. Use the number represented by each box.

• How many copies of Astonishing Force were sold?

_____

• How many copies of Team Amazing were sold? Explain.

_____

_____

_____

 Turn and Talk How can you show that your answer is correct
by using inverse operations?

Step It Out

2 The comic book store also sells collectible toys. The Gigantic Kid costs 4 times as much as the Marvelous Marvin. The Hall of Heroes playset costs 7 times as much as the Marvelous Marvin. If the three toys cost $1,044, how much does the Gigantic Kid cost?

A. Represent the situation with a bar model.

B. Write an equation to find the amount represented by each box of the bar model. Then find the number.

_____

C. Write an equation to find the cost of the Gigantic Kid. How much does the Gigantic Kid cost?

_____

Check Understanding Math Board

1 The amount of salt that a truck put on a road after a snowstorm in January was 14 times as much as the amount used in a February storm. The total amount of salt used was 4,230 pounds.

• Represent the situation with a bar model.

• How many pounds of salt were used in the January storm?

_____

On Your Own

2 (MP) **Use Structure** Tina's taco truck sold 3 times as many veggie tacos in August than in September. She sold twice as many in September than in October. She sold 927 veggie tacos during the three months.

- Represent the number of veggie tacos sold with a bar model.

- Write an equation to show the amount represented by each box of the bar model. Then find the amount.

  _____

- How many veggie tacos did Tina sell in September? Explain how you know.

  _____

  _____

3 (MP) **Model with Mathematics** Brody and his father catch an amberjack that weighs 54 pounds. Brody's mother catches a blue marlin that weighs 432 pounds. How many times as much does the marlin weigh as the amberjack?

- Represent the situation with a bar model.

- Write an equation to model the situation. How many times as much does the marlin weigh as the amberjack?

  _____

On Your Own

4 (MP) **Use Repeated Reasoning** Three farmers buy a total of 2,249 acres of land at an auction. Farmer Mel buys land that is 3 times as many acres as Farmer Cassius's land. Farmer Cassius buys land that is 3 times as many acres as Farmer Anne's land. How many acres of land does each farmer buy?

_____

_____

5 (MP) **Model with Mathematics** A local group raised $3,273 during a recent event. The money raised will be shared equally among 3 different charities. How much money will each charity receive? Write an equation to model the situation. Then solve.

_____

6 (MP) **Model with Mathematics** Mrs. Taylor owns a rectangular piece of land that has an area of 5,040 square feet. If the width of the piece of land is 48 feet, what is the length? Write an equation to model the situation. Then solve.

_____

7 (MP) **Model with Mathematics** A comic store sells two rare comic books for $1,824. The price of one comic book is 11 times as much as the price of the other.

- Write an equation to model the price of the less expensive comic book. Then find the price.

_____

- Write an equation to model the price of the more expensive comic book. Then find the price.

_____

Module 3

Review

Concepts and Skills

1 (MP) **Use Tools** The county theater has 24 equal rows of seats and has enough seats for 312 people. How many seats are in each row? Tell what strategy or tool you will use to answer the question, explain your choice, and then find the answer.

_____

2 Select all the expressions that have a value equal to 21.

(A) 888 ÷ 41

(D) 1,072 ÷ 49

(B) 945 ÷ 45

(E) 1,113 ÷ 53

(C) 1,010 ÷ 47

3 A factory makes 3,200 nails each day. Machines put 45 of these nails into each box of nails that the company sells, and these machines fill as many boxes as possible. How many boxes are filled, and how many nails are left over each day?

_____

4 Mrs. Cadle is saving to buy a racing bicycle. The bicycle costs $249, and she plans to save $20.00 each week. In how many weeks will she have saved enough money to buy the bicycle?
Explain your reasoning.

_____

Divide. Interpret the remainder to solve.

5 An adventure club is taking buses for a camping trip. If each bus can hold 44 members, how many buses will be needed for 334 members?

6 A satellite takes 28 days to travel around the planet. How many complete orbits does the satellite make every 365 days?

_____ _____

7 A grain silo contains 1,330 tons of corn. The corn will be divided equally among 42 trucks. To find the amount of corn in each truck, Eliot tries to solve 1,330 ÷ 42. He estimates that the first digit of the whole-number quotient will be 2 tens. How should he adjust the first digit?

(A) adjust it up to 3 tens

(C) adjust it up to 2 hundreds

(B) adjust it down to 1 ten

(D) adjust it down to 2 ones

Describe the estimated digit in the whole-number quotient as _too high_, _too low_, or _correct_. Adjust the estimated digit if needed. Then divide.

8
$$\begin{array}{r} 9 \\ 91\overline{)8{,}645} \end{array}$$

9
$$\begin{array}{r} 6 \\ 21\overline{)1{,}243} \end{array}$$

_____   _____

10 A musical group performs two concerts. A total of 512 people attend the two concerts. The bar model represents the number of people that attend each concert. Which expression models the number of people attending Concert 1?

Concert 1 [ ]

Concert 2 [ ][ ][ ][ ][ ]

(A) 512 ÷ 4

(C) 512 ÷ 6

(B) 512 ÷ 5

(D) 512 ÷ 7

11 Melanie had 8 times as many online customers as in-person customers today. She draws a bar model to compare the numbers of each type. If she served 234 customers today, how many online customers did she have?

In-person [ ]

Online [ ][ ][ ][ ][ ][ ][ ][ ]

(A) 26

(C) 182

(B) 156

(D) 208

Expressions

Can **Numbers** Do Magic Tricks?

- Follow the steps.

 A. Choose a number from 1 to 100. _____

 B. Multiply the number by 3. _____

 C. Add 21 to the number from Step B. _____

 D. Divide the sum in Step C by 3. _____

 E. Subtract the original number from

 the result of Step D. _____

 Turn and Talk

- Compare your starting number with other students. Then compare the resulting number. What were the results?

- Why do you think this trick works?

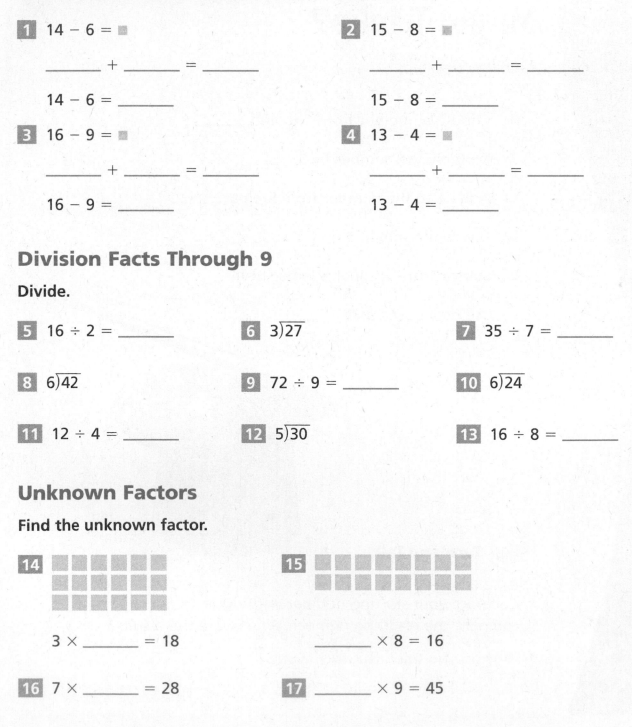

Are You Ready?

Complete these problems to review prior concepts and skills you will need for this module.

Think Addition to Subtract

Write a related addition fact to help you subtract.

1 14 − 6 = ▪

_____ + _____ = _____

14 − 6 = _____

2 15 − 8 = ▪

_____ + _____ = _____

15 − 8 = _____

3 16 − 9 = ▪

_____ + _____ = _____

16 − 9 = _____

4 13 − 4 = ▪

_____ + _____ = _____

13 − 4 = _____

Division Facts Through 9

Divide.

5 16 ÷ 2 = _____

6 3)‾27‾

7 35 ÷ 7 = _____

8 6)‾42‾

9 72 ÷ 9 = _____

10 6)‾24‾

11 12 ÷ 4 = _____

12 5)‾30‾

13 16 ÷ 8 = _____

Unknown Factors

Find the unknown factor.

14

3 × _____ = 18

15

_____ × 8 = 16

16 7 × _____ = 28

17 _____ × 9 = 45

Name _____

Write Numerical Expressions

(**I Can**) write a numerical expression to model a real-world situation, and I can interpret a numerical expression.

Spark Your Learning

A drum line is made up of 14 fourth-grade drummers and 12 fifth-grade drummers. The fourth-grade drummers stand in a line, and the fifth-grade drummers stand in a line behind them.

Draw a visual model of the situation. Describe how you can represent how many more drummers are in fourth grade than in fifth grade.

SMALL GROUPS

 Turn and Talk How do you know which operation to use for a situation?

Build Understanding

1 Every day Thora practices each page of this music 6 times.

Draw a visual model to show the number of pages Thora practices each day. Explain your visual model.

A. Which operation describes the situation? How do you know?

_____

_____

B. How can you model the number of pages of music Thora practices each day using a

numerical expression? _____

C. Describe what the numbers and operation sign in your numerical expression represent.

_____

_____

 Turn and Talk How would the expression change if Thora practices the same number of pages for 5 days?

2 Mr. Lopez bought a snack 2 times this week while watching the drum line practice. Both days he started with the same amount of money and had $3 left after he bought his snack.

A. How can you model the amount of money Mr. Lopez spent in one day? Write a numerical expression.

_____

B. How can you model the amount of money he spent on snacks? Write a numerical expression for each day.

_____

C. How can you model the amount of money he spent in 2 days using a single numerical expression? Use two operation signs and parentheses in your numerical expression.

_____

D. How do you know where to place the parentheses in your numerical expression?

_____

_____

 Turn and Talk Suppose there were no parentheses in your numerical expression from Part C. Would the answer be the same? Why or why not?

• •

Check Understanding [Math Board]

Write a numerical expression to model the situation.

1 Beverly has 2 pens. She buys 1 more pen.

2 Two students share 8 markers equally.

_____   _____

On Your Own

3 (MP) **Model with Mathematics** Fifteen ensembles, or groups of musicians, perform in the summer parade. Each group has the same number of performers as shown. Write a numerical expression that models the total number of performers in the parade.

_____

Write a numerical expression to model the words.

4 Add 28 and 15.

5 Subtract 1 from 12 and then multiply the difference by 4.

_____   _____

6 (MP) **Reason** Clarence deletes 1 of 17 folders of photos from a computer. He puts an equal number of the remaining folders onto two computer drives. Write a numerical expression to model the situation. How do you know your answer is correct?

_____

_____

_____

_____

✦ I'm in a Learning Mindset!

What is still unclear about numerical expressions?

_____

_____

_____

Name

Interpret Numerical Expressions

(I Can) compare numerical expressions which are written with one expression in terms of the other.

Spark Your Learning

Michel and Sandra belong to a Remote-Control Club. They replace the batteries in their cars once a week. How does the number of batteries Michel and Sandra use in 3 weeks compare to the number of batteries they use in 1 week?

Compare the number of batteries they use. Draw to show your thinking.

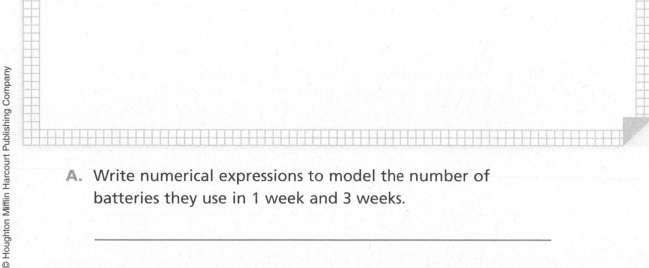

A. Write numerical expressions to model the number of batteries they use in 1 week and 3 weeks.

_____

 Turn and Talk How can you check if your numerical expression is correct?

Build Understanding

1 The Remote-Control Club has two runways
where airplanes take off. The sizes of
the runways are shown on the map.

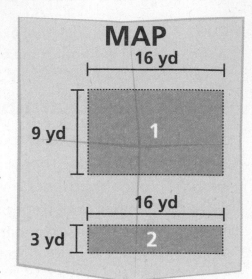

A. How can you model the area of
Runway 1 using a numerical expression?

_____

B. How can you model the area of Runway 2
using a numerical expression?

_____

C. Describe the length of each runway.

_____

D. Compare the widths of the runways. Explain how you know.

_____

_____

E. Compare the areas of the runways without evaluating them.

_____

_____

F. Compare the numerical expressions that model the area
of each runway. Explain your reasoning.

_____

_____

_____

 Turn and Talk Runway 1 will be expanded from
16 yards long to 32 yards long. How will the area of the
expanded Runway 1 compare to the area of Runway 2?

© Houghton Mifflin Harcourt Publishing Company

2 Mr. Liu follows the directions shown when he flies his remote-control airplanes.

Directions
Add 15 mL of oil daily.

Add 5 mL of oil for each flight.

6   7

A. How can you model the amount of oil he needs for one flight of one airplane using a numerical expression?

_____

B. How can you model the amount of oil he needs for one flight of four airplanes using a numerical expression?

_____

C. How do your numerical expressions from Parts A and B compare? Explain how you know.

_____

_____

_____

• •

Check Understanding 🔲 Math Board

1 Each month for 2 months, Kyle buys a pack of 8 replacement tires for his remote-control car. At the end of each month, he has 1 tire left. Explain how the numerical expression for the number of tires Kyle uses in 2 months compares to the numerical expression for the number of tires he uses in 1 month.

_____

_____

Compare the numerical expressions.

2 28 × 6 and 14 × 6

_____

_____

3 3 × (8 + 6) and 8 + 6

_____

_____

On Your Own

4  **(MP) Critique Reasoning** James is making banners for his club's airplanes to pull. Each banner is 5 feet long and is attached by a 10-foot long rope. He models the total length of the banners and rope for six airplanes with the numerical expression 6 × (5 + 10). He says the total length for six planes is five times as great as the total length needed for one plane. Correct his error.

_____

_____

Compare the numerical expressions.

5 33 + 67 and 9 × (33 + 67)

_____

_____

6 4 × (2,101 − 987) and 2,101 − 987

_____

_____

7 **(MP) Reason** Explain how 56 × 9 compares to 8 × 9.

_____

_____

✛ I'm in a Learning Mindset!

What questions can I ask my peers to help me understand how to interpret numerical expressions?

_____

_____

Name _____

Evaluate Numerical Expressions

(I Can) evaluate a numerical expression using the order of operations.

Spark Your Learning

Mr. North's music club writes a song together. Each verse of the song has 6 lines, and each chorus has 2 lines. If the song has 4 verses and choruses, how many lines does the song have in all?

Draw a visual model to show the problem. Explain your reasoning.

SMALL GROUPS

Turn and Talk Think about a numerical expression that models the number of lines in the song. If the song is shortened from 4 verses and choruses to 3, how does the numerical expression and its value change?

Build Understanding

1 A club is making a music video. A group of 12 singers perform the first verse. Three different groups of 6 singers perform the other 3 verses. The numerical expression $12 + 3 \times 6$ models the situation. How many singers are making the music video?

A. Which operations are modeled in the numerical expression?

_____

B. When you evaluate the numerical expression, which operation should be done first? How do you know?

_____

_____

_____

C. Describe how to evaluate $12 + 3 \times 6$.

_____

_____

D. Evaluate the numerical expression, then explain what your answer means in this situation.

_____

_____

E. How many singers are making the music video?

_____

 Turn and Talk Why do the two expressions $(12 + 3) \times 6$ and $12 + 3 \times 6$ have different values?

© Houghton Mifflin Harcourt Publishing Company

Connect to Vocabulary

To **evaluate** a numerical expression, find its value by carrying out all of its operations in the correct order.

The **order of operations** is a set of rules for evaluating a numerical expression.

The order of operations is:
1. Perform operations in parentheses.
2. Multiply and divide from left to right.
3. Add and subtract from left to right.

Step It Out

2 The club members spend 4 hours rehearsing and 2 hours filming a music video for 3 Saturdays. The numerical expression $(4 + 2) \times 3$ can be used to model the situation.

A. Rewrite $(4 + 2) \times 3$ using repeated addition, then evaluate.

_____

B. Rewrite $(4 + 2) \times 3$ using the Distributive Property, then evaluate.

_____

C. Use the order of operations to evaluate $(4 + 2) \times 3$. How many hours do the club members spend making the video?

_____

 Turn and Talk How do the methods you used to evaluate the numerical expression compare?

Check Understanding [Math Board]

1 Ervin evaluates $12 \div (2 + 4) + 6 \times 3$ by first dividing $12 \div 2$ and then multiplying 6×3. Then, he adds from left to right. Explain his errors.

_____

_____

Evaluate the numerical expression.

2 $4 \times (15 - 7) + 8$

3 $12 \times 12 + 7 \times 8 + 5$

On Your Own

4 (MP) **Model with Mathematics** Ms. Garcia has 120 comic books. She gives 15 to each of her three nephews, then buys 4 more. Write and evaluate a numerical expression that describes the number of comic books she has now.

_____

Evaluate the numerical expression.

5 $35 - 5 \times (12 - 7)$

_____

6 $12 + 6 \div 3 + 3$

_____

7 $18 \div 6 + 12 - 1$

_____

8 $3 + 9 \times 8 - 4$

_____

9 Consider the expression $(4 \times 3 - 1) \times 5$. For a numerical expression with multiple operations in the same set of parentheses, in which order should you perform the operations? Evaluate this expression.

_____

_____

_____

_____

© Houghton Mifflin Harcourt Publishing Company

🔳 I'm in a Learning Mindset!

What is different about trying to evaluate a numerical expression with a partner than trying to solve it on my own? Which do I prefer?

_____

_____

Name _____

Use Grouping Symbols

(I Can) describe how to use grouping symbols in a numerical expression and place parentheses so an expression has a given value.

Step It Out

1 Justine is making jewelry for her friends. She makes 4 of the bracelets shown. To determine the number of beads she needs, she writes the numerical expression $5 + 3 + 6 \times 4$.

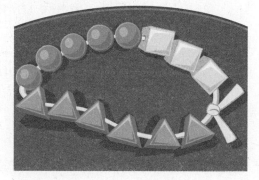

A. Use the order of operations to evaluate Justine's numerical expression.

_____

B. Which part of Justine's numerical expression models the number of beads she uses for 1 bracelet?

_____

C. How can you use your answer from Part B to find how many beads she uses for 4 bracelets?

_____

D. How many beads does she need to make 4 bracelets? How does your answer compare to the answer you found in Part A?

_____

E. How can you rewrite $5 + 3 + 6 \times 4$ with parentheses so that it models the number of beads she needs to make 4 bracelets?

_____

 Turn and Talk Where can you place one pair of parentheses in the numerical expression $5 \times 8 - 4 + 2$ to get the least possible value? Explain how you know.

Step It Out

brackets

parentheses

braces

2 Mr. Finn makes gift boxes with 4 green bracelets, 1 gold bracelet, and 1 necklace. Each bracelet costs $2 to make, and each necklace costs $5. He has $90 to spend on gift boxes. How can you model the number of gift boxes Mr. Finn can make using a numerical expression?

A. Parentheses ( ): Write an expression in parentheses to represent the total number of bracelets in one gift box.

(_____ + _____)

B. Brackets [ ]: Write an expression in brackets to represent the total cost of the bracelets in one gift box.

[_____ × (_____ + _____)]

C. Braces { }: Write an expression in braces to represent the total cost of the bracelets and the necklace in one gift box.

{[_____ × (_____ + _____)] + _____}

D. Write and evaluate an expression to show how many gift boxes Mr. Finn can make with $90.

_____ ÷ {[_____ × (_____ + _____)] + _____}

_____

 Turn and Talk Look at the placement of the parentheses, brackets, and braces. How would you describe to someone the order of evaluating based on their position?

• •

Check Understanding **Math Board**

1 Liza is making 3 necklaces. Each necklace has 4 pink beads, 6 purple beads, and 10 blue beads. Use parentheses to rewrite the numerical expression 3 × 4 + 6 + 10 so that it models the number of beads Liza needs to make 3 necklaces.

_____

On Your Own

2 (MP) **Model with Mathematics** During a conference, a group makes the same lunch order shown in the table each day for 4 days. Use parentheses to rewrite the numerical expression to have a value of $308.

$4 \times 8 \times 6 + 7 \times 2 + 3 \times 5$

Item	Number of Items	Cost for Each Item
Sandwich	8	$6
Fruit	7	$2
Salad	3	$5

_____

3 (MP) **Reason** When the numerical expression $80 - 20 \div 4$ is rewritten with parentheses, it can have a value of 15 or 75. Explain.

_____

_____

_____

_____

_____

Use parentheses to rewrite the expression to have the given value.

4 $7 \times 5 - 4 + 2$

value: 9

_____

5 $8 + 12 \div 4 + 2$

value: 10

_____

6 $2 + 6 \times 5 - 4$

value: 36

_____

7 $2 + 7 - 2 \times 4$

value: 22

_____

8 $90 - 30 \div 6$

value: 10

_____

9 $12 + 24 \div 6 - 3$

value: 3

_____

On Your Own

10 (MP) **Model with Mathematics** Nayla works at a health food store. The store has the bins shown. On Monday, the bins are full. The store sells 13 pounds of granola by Friday. Nayla wants to evenly divide the remaining granola in the 7 bins. Use parentheses to rewrite the numerical expression to model the amount that will be in each bin, 2 pounds.

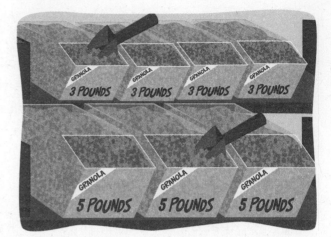

$4 \times 3 + 3 \times 5 - 13 \div 7$

_____

11 (MP) **Critique Reasoning** Deshawn says that he can evaluate the numerical expression $7 + (3 \times 8) - 5$ without parentheses and get the same answer. Is Deshawn correct? Explain how you know.

_____

_____

_____

_____

12 (MP) **Reason** Describe how you would evaluate the numerical expression $48 \div \{[2 \times (1 + 3)] + 4\}$.

_____

_____

_____

13 (MP) **Reason** Use parentheses to rewrite $16 + 4 \times 4 - 3$ to have a value of 20. Then rewrite the expression to have a value of 77.

_____

_____

Name _____

Review

Vocabulary

1 Draw lines to match the term with its description.

evaluate •

numerical expression •

order of operations •

• to find the value of a numerical expression

• a special set of rules which gives the order in which calculations are done in a numerical expression

• a mathematical phrase that uses only numbers and operation signs

Concepts and Skills

2 Write a numerical expression to model the words.

Add 5 and 25, and then multiply the sum by 4.

_____

3 Which of the following can be modeled by the numerical expression $(20 - 15) \div 5$? Select all that apply.

(A) Find the difference of 20 and the quotient of 15 and 5.

(B) Subtract 15 from 20, and then divide the difference by 5.

(C) Divide 20 by 5, and then subtract 15.

(D) Divide the difference of 20 and 15 by 5.

(E) Subtract the quotient of 15 and 5 from 20.

4 **(MP) Use Tools** Compare the numerical expressions $9 \times (15 - 8)$ and $15 - 8$. Tell what strategy or tool you will use to solve the problem, explain your choice, and then find the answer.

_____

_____

5 Which is the value of the numerical expression $6 + 2 \times (8 - 4)$?

Ⓐ 10

Ⓑ 12

Ⓒ 14

Ⓓ 32

6 Which is the value of the numerical expression $30 \div 5 - (3 + 1)$?

Ⓐ 2

Ⓑ 4

Ⓒ 16

Ⓓ 30

7 Select all the numerical expressions that have a value of 9.

Ⓐ $6 \times (5 + 2 \times 9 - 3)$

Ⓑ $6 \times 5 - 2 \times 9 - 3$

Ⓒ $6 \times (5 - 2) \times 9 - 3$

Ⓓ $(6 \times 5 - 2) \times 9 + 3$

Ⓔ $(6 \times 5) - (2 \times 9) - 3$

Ⓕ $(6 \times 5) - 2 \times (9 - 3)$

8 Use parentheses to rewrite the numerical expression $18 + 3 \times 6 \div 3$ to have a value of 12.

_____

9 Use parentheses to rewrite the numerical expression $4 \times 7 - 2 \times 3$ to have a value of 60.

_____

© Houghton Mifflin Harcourt Publishing Company

How can I **cover** this stain?

- Oh no! There is a stain on the wooden floor. Draw the smallest rectangular carpet you can use to cover the stain.

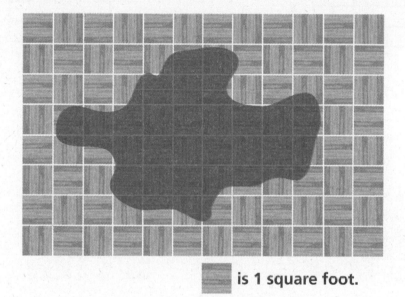

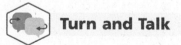 **is 1 square foot.**

- What is the length of your rectangle?

_____

- What is the width of your rectangle?

_____

- What is the area of the carpet you used?

_____

Turn and Talk

- How many 1-foot-by-1-foot pieces of carpet do you need to cover only the stain? Explain your thinking.

Are You Ready?

Complete these problems to review prior concepts and skills you will need for this module.

Perimeter

Find the perimeter.

1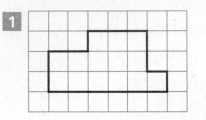

Perimeter = _____ units

2

Perimeter = _____ units

Area

Count to find the area of the figure.

3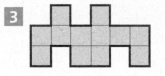

Area = _____ square units

4

Area = _____ square units

Use the Associative Property of Multiplication

Find the unknown number.

5 $4 \times 80 = (4 \times \text{_____}) \times 10$

6 $3 \times 50 = (3 \times \text{_____}) \times 10$

7 $6 \times 70 = (6 \times \text{_____}) \times 10$

8 $60 \times 9 = 10 \times (\text{_____} \times 9)$

9 $30 \times 7 = 10 \times (\text{_____} \times 7)$

10 $4 \times 40 = (4 \times \text{_____}) \times 10$

© Houghton Mifflin Harcourt Publishing Company

Name
_____

Use Unit Cubes to Build Solid Figures

(I Can) build solid figures using unit cubes.

Spark Your Learning

Alexandra is volunteering to stack boxes of soup cans at a community food bank. She stacks the boxes to form the right rectangular prism shown. Make visual models to show three other ways that Alexandra can stack the boxes to form right rectangular prisms.

Describe your visual models.

SMALL GROUPS

Turn and Talk In what other ways can Alexandra stack the 12 boxes?

Build Understanding

1 Carlos and Kelly are building store displays in the shape of **right rectangular prisms** using cube-shaped boxes of the same size.

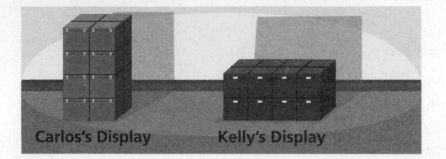

Carlos's Display   Kelly's Display

A. Use unit cubes to make visual models of the two displays.

B. How many cubes are in each visual model?

_____

C. Think of the length of the edge of each cube-shaped box as one unit. What are the **dimensions** of each display?

_____

_____

D. How many **faces** and **edges** does a unit cube have?

_____

E. How many faces and edges does each display have?

_____

F. How can you place Carlos's display to make it match Kelly's display exactly?

_____

Turn and Talk How can you tell how many unit cubes make up a right rectangular prism if you cannot see all the unit cubes that make it up?

© Houghton Mifflin Harcourt Publishing Company

Connect to Vocabulary

A cube is a type of right rectangular prism. A **unit cube** is a cube that has a length, width, and height of 1 unit.

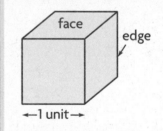

face

edge

←1 unit→

---

2 For a concert, Angela builds platforms using cube-shaped blocks, each with an edge of 1 unit.

A. Use unit cubes to build a visual model of each platform. How many unit cubes are in each visual model?

_____

_____

B. Which platform has the greatest number of blocks?

_____

 Turn and Talk How many other platforms can you design using 5 unit cubes? Describe how the platforms are the same and different.

Check Understanding [Math Board]

Aron builds store displays using cube-shaped boxes. Count the number of unit cubes used to build the solid figure.

1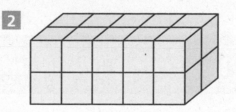

2

_____   _____

On Your Own

3 (MP) **Reason** Using cube-shaped mini cakes of the same size, a pastry chef creates the larger cake shown for a party. If each mini cake serves one guest, how many servings are in the larger cake? Explain how you know.

_____

_____

_____

_____

4 **Open Ended** Describe two different right rectangular prisms that can be made using 18 unit cubes.

_____

_____

Count the number of unit cubes used to build each solid figure.

5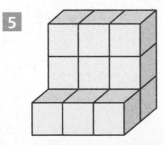

6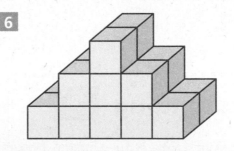

_____   _____

💠 I'm in a Learning Mindset!

What is still unclear about the relationship between rectangular prisms and unit cubes?

_____

Name _____

Understand Volume

(I Can) use unit cubes to find the volume of a
right rectangular prism.

Spark Your Learning

A toy company's engineers determine that the best
way to package number cubes with a 1-unit length
into a single box is to stack them in the shape of a
right rectangular prism. How many different kinds
of right rectangular prisms could this number of
cubes be stacked in?

Describe the different right rectangular prisms.

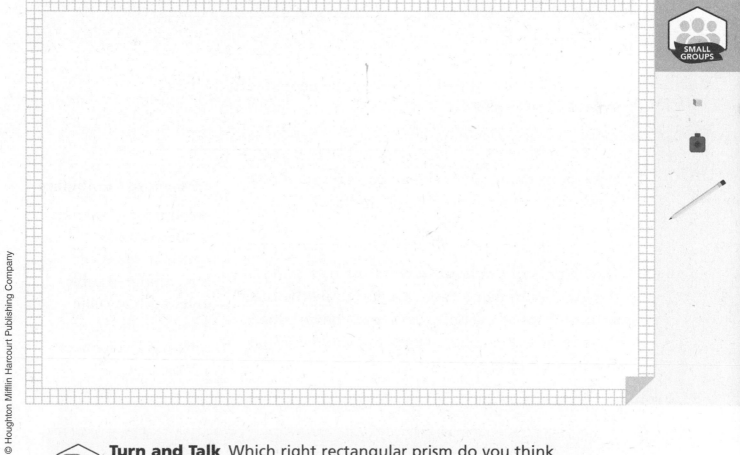

SMALL
GROUPS

Turn and Talk Which right rectangular prism do you think
would be the best for packaging the number cubes? Give
reasons to support your answer.

© Houghton Mifflin Harcourt Publishing Company

Build Understanding

1 The picture shows a box designed to pack game cubes. Each game cube is the size of a unit cube.

A. How many game cubes can be packed into the bottom layer of the box with no gaps or overlaps? Explain how you know.

_____

_____

B. How many layers of game cubes can be packed into the box? How do you know?

_____

C. How many game cubes can be packed so the box is full and there are no gaps or overlaps?

_____

D. The volume of the box can be found by finding the number of game cubes it takes to fill the box with no gaps or overlaps. Since each game cube is the size of a unit cube, what is the volume of the box in cubic units?

_____

> **Connect to Vocabulary**
>
> **Volume** is the amount of space a solid figure occupies and is measured in **cubic units**, such as cubic inches (cu in.). A unit cube has a volume of 1 cubic unit.

Turn and Talk How are the number of cubes in one layer and the number of layers related to the volume of the box?

2 A craft store packages cube-shaped beads as shown. Each bead measures 1 centimeter along each edge. There are no gaps or overlaps in the package.

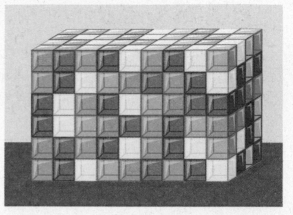

A. How many beads are shown? Explain how you know.

_____

_____

B. What is the volume of the box in cubic centimeters? _____

C. Suppose each bead measures 1 inch on each edge. What would be the volume of the box in cubic inches? _____

Turn and Talk Would the box be the same size if it were filled with an equal amount of centimeter cubes or foot cubes? Explain.

Check Understanding [Math Board]

1 A warehouse receives a shipment of cube-shaped boxes that measure 1 foot along each edge. If the boxes are stacked to form the right rectangular prism shown, what is the volume of the prism?

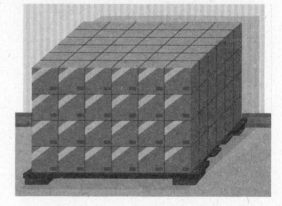

_____

2 Use the unit given. Find the volume.

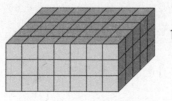

1 unit [cube] 1 unit
1 unit   1 unit

_____

On Your Own

3 **(MP)** **Use Structure** A puzzle consists of blocks made from 1-inch cubes as shown. What is the volume of the right rectangular prism? Explain how you know.

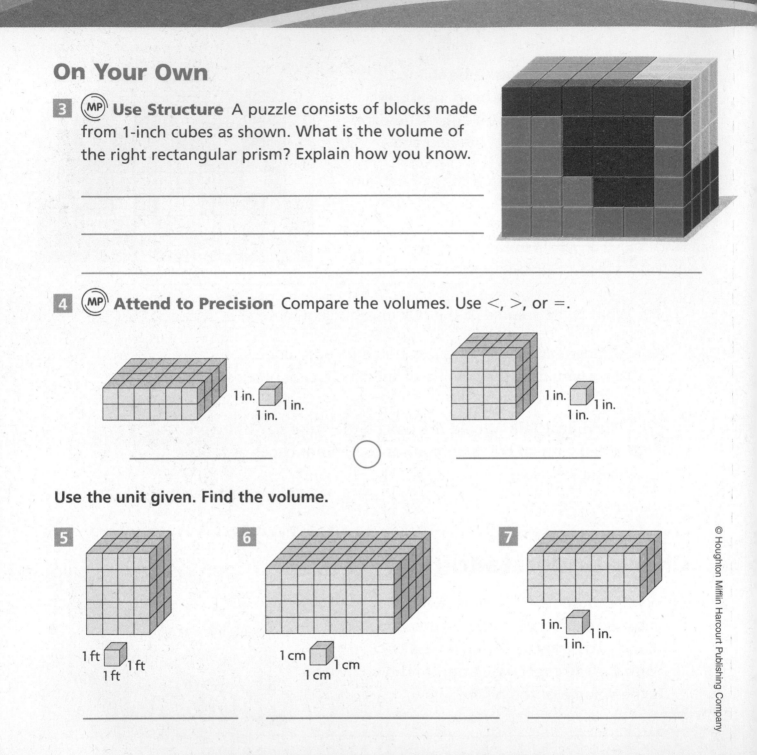

_____

_____

_____

4 **(MP)** **Attend to Precision** Compare the volumes. Use <, >, or =.

1 in. 1 in. 1 in.

1 in. 1 in. 1 in.

_____ ◯ _____

Use the unit given. Find the volume.

5

1 ft 1 ft 1 ft

_____

6

1 cm 1 cm 1 cm

_____

7

1 in. 1 in. 1 in.

_____

⬡ I'm in a Learning Mindset!

How did using unit cubes help me understand how to find the volume?

_____

_____

Name

Estimate Volume

(I Can) use an everyday object to estimate the volume of a
right rectangular prism.

Spark Your Learning

Nicole is sending care packages
to troops overseas. She places
boxes of cards of the same size
into a large box as shown.

**Estimate how many boxes of cards Nicole can place in the large box.
How do you know?**

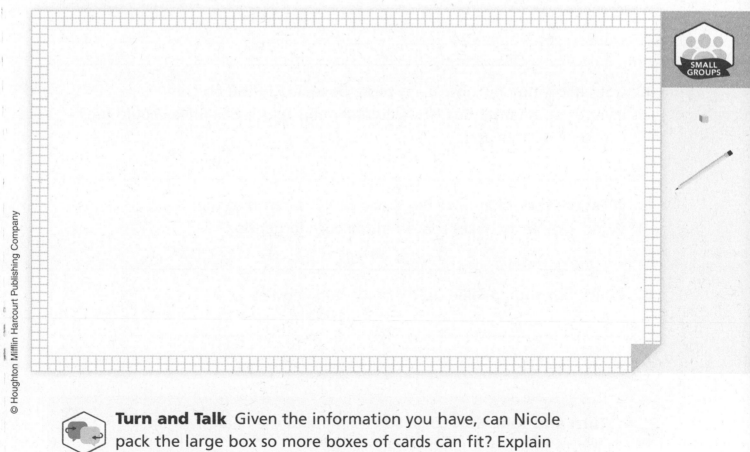

SMALL
GROUPS

Turn and Talk Given the information you have, can Nicole
pack the large box so more boxes of cards can fit? Explain
your thinking.

Build Understanding

1 Billie packs pasta boxes into one of two larger boxes for a local food bank. If she wants to pack at least 29 pasta boxes in one of the larger boxes, which box should she use?

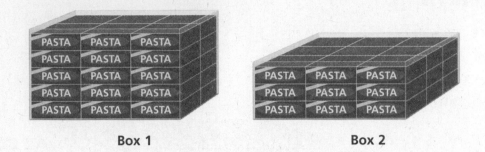

Box 1   Box 2

A. How many pasta boxes are shown in the bottom layer of each larger box? How do you know?

_____

_____

_____

B. Does knowing only how many pasta boxes are in the bottom layer of each larger box help you determine which box Billie should use? Explain your thinking.

_____

C. What are the volumes of Box 1 and Box 2 in terms of the number of pasta boxes that fit inside each larger box?

_____

D. Which box should Billie use? How do you know?

_____

_____

 Turn and Talk How could you estimate to the nearest whole unit to find the volume of each larger box?

2 A company sends boxes of phones from its warehouse. The volume of each phone and its protective packaging is 12 cubic inches.

A. How many phones are in the bottom layer? _____

B. How many layers are shown in the box?

_____

C. How many phones are in the box? _____

D. How can you estimate the volume of the box?

_____

_____

E. Estimate the volume of the box of phones. _____

Turn and Talk How can you estimate the volume of a box that is packed with 4 fewer phones in each layer?

• •

Check Understanding [Math Board]

Estimate the volume of the large box.

1 Volume of watch box: 40 cu cm

_____

2 Volume of action figure box: 60 cu in.

_____

On Your Own

3 (MP) **Use Structure** A large box is packed with 6 rows of 8 boxes of dried cranberries in the bottom layer. The box is about 4 layers high. Estimate the volume of the large box if each box of dried cranberries has a volume of 16 cubic inches.

_____

4 (MP) **Reason** Boxes 1 and 2 are packed with small boxes that are all the same size. They each have a volume of about 8 cubic inches. How do the volumes of Box 1 and Box 2 compare?

_____

_____

Box 1

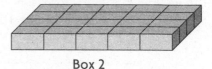

Box 2

Estimate the volume of the large box.

5 Volume of jump rope box: 3 cu ft

_____

6 Volume of pencil box: 25 cu cm

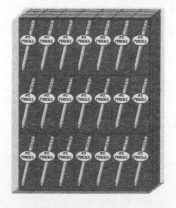

_____

© Houghton Mifflin Harcourt Publishing Company

🔷 I'm in a Learning Mindset!

Who should I talk with to learn more about estimating volume?

_____

_____

Name _____

Find Volume of Right Rectangular Prisms

(I Can) find the volume of a right rectangular prism using the area of the base and the height.

Spark Your Learning

For his junior engineering club, Miguel is designing a box in the shape of a right rectangular prism that can hold exactly 12 one-inch number cubes with no extra space.

What are the dimensions and volume of a box Miguel can design? Justify your reasoning.

Turn and Talk Compare the possible dimensions of the different boxes Miguel can design. How are they related to the number of cubes?

© Houghton Mifflin Harcourt Publishing Company

Build Understanding

1 Naomi works at a health food company. She needs to stack 1-inch protein cubes into a box as shown with no extra space.

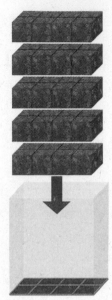

A. What is the area of the base of the box?

_____

B. What is the volume for one layer of cubes? Explain how you know.

_____

_____

C. How is the volume of the prism different from the area of the base it is sitting on?

_____

_____

D. As each layer is added on top of the base layer, how does the volume change?

_____

E. Complete the table to find the volume of Naomi's box. How is the volume related to the height?

Height (in layers)	1	2	3	4	5
Volume (in cubic inches)					

_____

F. What is the volume of Naomi's box? _____

 Turn and Talk How can you use the terms length, width, and height to describe how to find the volume of the box? How can you use the height and the area of the base to find the volume of the box?

Step It Out

2 Angela is a culinary artist. She wants to pack the 1-centimeter food cubes into a container as shown.

A. What is the volume of one food cube? How do you know?

_____

_____

_____

B. How many 1-centimeter food cubes will she pack into the container? How can you use this amount to find the volume of the container?

_____

_____

C. What is the area of the base of the container that Angela needs?

_____

D. What is the height of the container?

_____

E. Write a numerical expression, using the height, to model the volume of the container.

_____

F. What is the volume of Angela's container? How does your answer compare to your answer from Part B?

_____

Turn and Talk Suppose Angela rearranges the food cubes so that the area of the base is 42 square centimeters. What will be the new height of the container? Describe how to find the volume of this container.

Step It Out

3 Angela rearranges her 1-centimeter food cubes as shown.

A. What are the length and width of the base?

_____

B. Write a numerical expression for the area of the base.

_____

C. What is the height? _____

D. Write a numerical expression for the volume.

_____

E. Use your expression to find the volume. How does your answer compare with the volume you found in Step It Out 2?

_____

 Turn and Talk How can you use the properties of multiplication to find the volume of the prism mentally?

Check Understanding Math Board

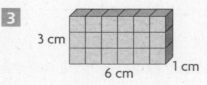

1 One layer of 1-centimeter bouillon cubes is shown. If 8 layers are stacked, what is the volume of the right rectangular prism formed by the stack?

_____

Find the volume.

2

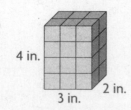

4 in.

3 in.

2 in.

3

3 cm

6 cm

1 cm

_____   _____

On Your Own

4 (MP) **Reason** Two layers of 1-inch cubes of cheese are placed on a platter as shown. If four more layers are added, what is the total volume of cheese? Explain how you know.

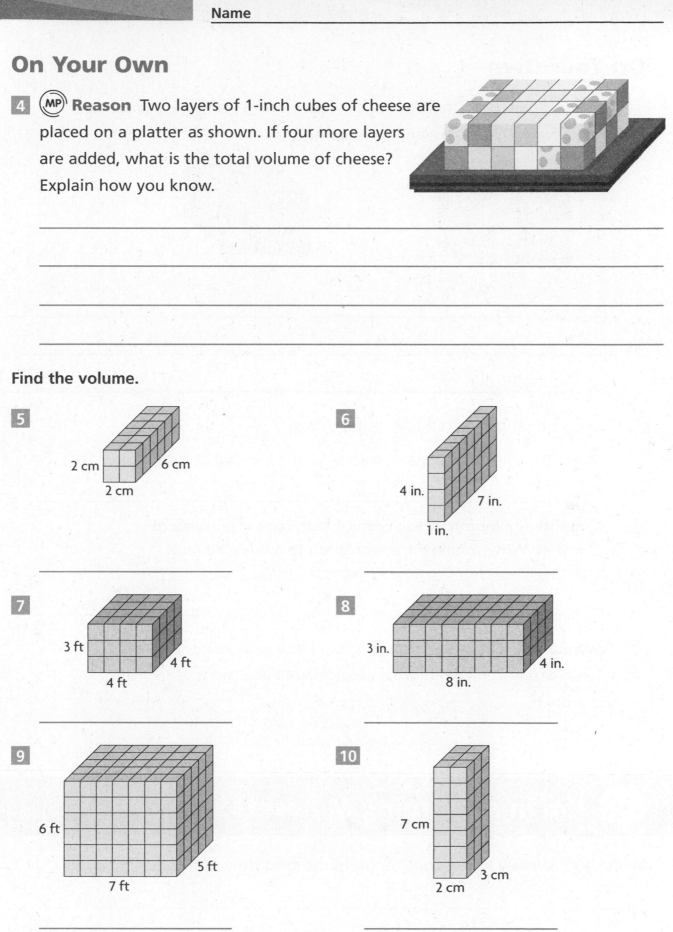

_____

_____

_____

_____

Find the volume.

5

2 cm   6 cm
2 cm

6

4 in.   7 in.
1 in.

7

3 ft   4 ft
4 ft

8

3 in.   4 in.
8 in.

9

6 ft   5 ft
7 ft

10

7 cm   3 cm
2 cm

On Your Own

11 (MP) **Use Structure** Danielle makes these displays using 1-inch blocks of wood. Which has the greater volume? Explain.

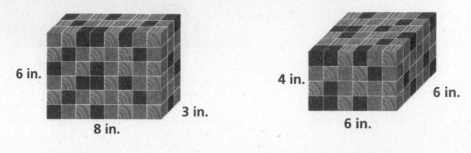

6 in.

3 in.

8 in.

4 in.

6 in.

6 in.

_____

_____

12 Consider the right rectangular prism shown.

• If the length of the edge of each cube is 1 inch, what is the volume?

_____

• Suppose the length of the edge of each cube is doubled to 2 inches. Write a numerical expression to model the new volume. Then find the new volume.

_____

13 **Open Ended** A right rectangular prism has a square base and a volume of 144 cubic feet. What are possible dimensions of the prism?

_____

⊹ I'm in a Learning Mindset!

What do I already know that can help me find the volume on my own?

_____

Name _____

Apply Volume Formulas

(I Can) use a formula to find the volume of a
right rectangular prism.

Step It Out

1 Jeanie buys the fish tank shown.

A. You know that the volume
of a rectangular prism can be
expressed as the product of its
length, width, and height. Write
a formula to model the volume
of a rectangular prism.

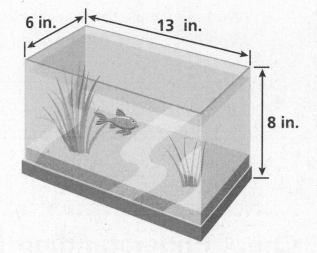

_____

B. Use the formula to write an
equation for the volume of
the tank.

_____

C. Multiply from left to right. What is the product of the
length and width?

_____

D. Multiply the product of the length and width by the height.
What is the volume of the fish tank?

_____

   Turn and Talk How can you use the Associative Property
of Multiplication to identify the part of the formula that
represents the area of the base of the rectangular prism?

2 ▶ Jeanie finds another fish tank in the shape of a right rectangular prism with the dimensions shown.

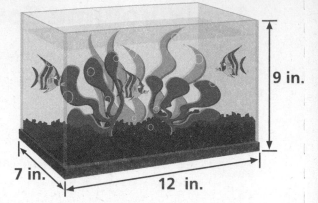

9 in.

7 in.

12 in.

A. Let *B* represent the base area of a right rectangular prism. What equation represents the base area of the fish tank?

_____

B. Write a formula to model the volume of a right rectangular prism using *B*.

_____

C. Use the formula to write an equation for the volume of the tank. What is the volume of the tank?

_____

Check Understanding Math Board

1 A storage unit is 12 feet wide, 8 feet long, and 9 feet high. What is the volume of the storage unit? _____

Find the volume.

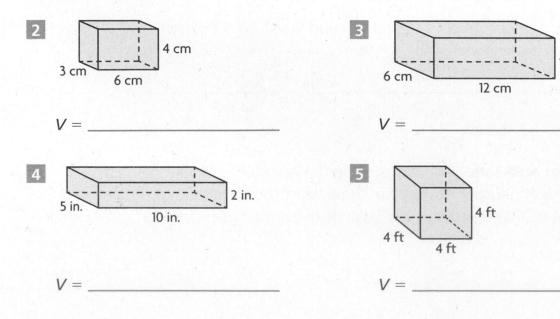

2

4 cm
3 cm
6 cm

V = _____

3

4 cm
6 cm
12 cm

V = _____

4

2 in.
5 in.
10 in.

V = _____

5

4 ft
4 ft
4 ft

V = _____

On Your Own

6 Zachary has a trunk with the dimensions shown. What is the volume of the trunk?

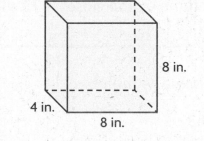

16 in.

13 in.

30 in.

_____

7 (MP) **Use Structure** A dresser is in the shape of a right rectangular prism. The area of the base is 6 square feet and the height is 4 feet. What is the volume of the dresser?

_____

Find the volume.

8

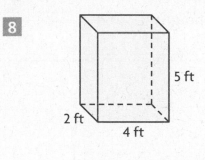

5 ft

2 ft

4 ft

V = _____

9

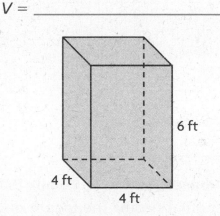

8 in.

4 in.

8 in.

V = _____

10

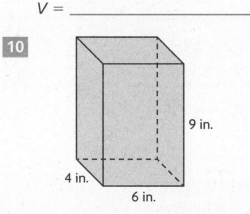

9 in.

4 in.

6 in.

V = _____

11

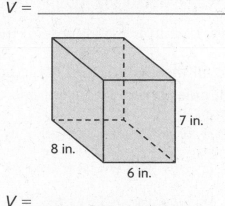

6 ft

4 ft

4 ft

V = _____

12

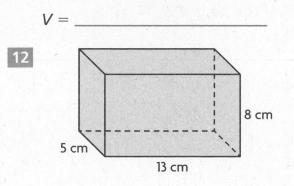

8 cm

5 cm

13 cm

V = _____

13

7 in.

8 in.

6 in.

V = _____

On Your Own

14 (MP) **Attend to Precision** Jason has gift boxes with the same dimensions as the one shown. He fits all of his boxes exactly into a larger box with a volume of 1,152 cubic inches. How many gift boxes are in the larger box? Explain how you know.

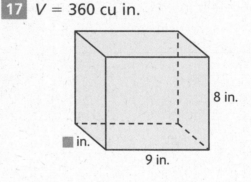
4 in.
4 in.
6 in.

_____

_____

15 (MP) **Reason** A closet is in the shape of a right rectangular prism. The area of the floor is 9 square feet. The volume of the closet is 72 cubic feet. What is the height

of the closet? _____

Find the unknown number.

16 V = 168 cu cm

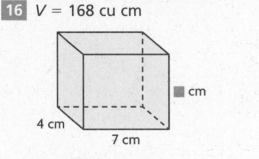
■ cm
4 cm
7 cm

17 V = 360 cu in.

8 in.
■ in.
9 in.

_____   _____

18 (MP) **Reason** Parma has a box that is in the shape of a right rectangular prism. The length of the box is twice the height. The length is 6 inches longer than the width. If the height is

8 inches, what is the volume of the box? _____

19 Circle all the options that could be the dimensions of a right rectangular prism with a volume of 192 cubic feet.

l = 8 ft, w = 6 ft, h = 4 ft   l = 6 ft, w = 6 ft, h = 8 ft

l = 8 ft, w = 3 ft, h = 8 ft   l = 4 ft, w = 3 ft, h = 16 ft

l = 5 ft, w = 4 ft, h = 12 ft   l = 10 ft, w = 6 ft, h = 4 ft

Name _____

Find Volume of Composed Figures

(I Can) find the volume of a figure composed of right
rectangular prisms.

Step It Out

1 Braydon builds a frame in the shape shown.
He plans to pour concrete into his frame.

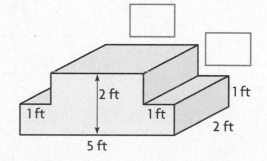

A. Write the unknown dimensions of the
composed figure. Describe how you
found your answers.

_____

_____

_____

B. Draw a line to show how you can break apart Braydon's
frame into two right rectangular prisms, and then find the
volume of each prism. Describe your answer.

_____

_____

_____

C. What is the amount of concrete that Braydon needs? Describe
how you found your answer.

_____

_____

_____

  Turn and Talk Is there another way to break apart the frame
into right rectangular prisms? Explain.

Step It Out

2 Tori wants to use the design shown to build steps from solid blocks of wood. Find the amount of wood she needs to build the steps.

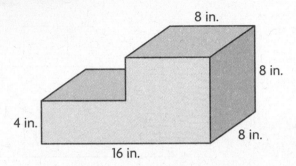

8 in.

8 in.

4 in.

8 in.

16 in.

A. Draw a line to show how you can break apart Tori's design into two right rectangular prisms, and then find the length, width, and height of each right rectangular prism.

_____

B. What is the volume of each of your rectangular prisms?

_____

C. Write an equation to model the amount of wood that Tori needs to build the steps.

_____

D. What is the amount of wood that Tori needs to build

the steps? _____

E. Describe how you can check your answer using unit cubes.

_____

_____

Turn and Talk Suppose Tori wants to make steps by cutting out wood in the shape of a right rectangular prism from a single block of wood. What could be the dimensions of the single block of wood?

3 Consider the space shown above Tori's bottom step.

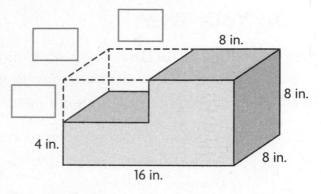

8 in.

8 in.

4 in.

8 in.

16 in.

A. Write the dimensions of the space above the bottom step, and then find the volume of the space.

_____

B. If the space and the steps are combined, they form a right rectangular prism. What are the dimensions of the prism, and what is its volume?

_____

_____

C. What is the volume when you subtract the volume of the space from the volume of the prism? What does it represent?

_____

_____

Turn and Talk Describe two ways to find the volume of a composed figure.

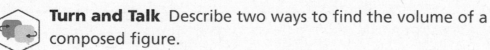

Check Understanding [Math Board]

Find the volume of the composed figure.

1

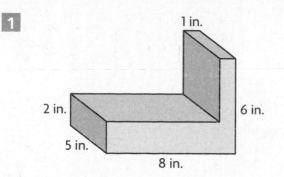

1 in.

2 in.

6 in.

5 in.

8 in.

2

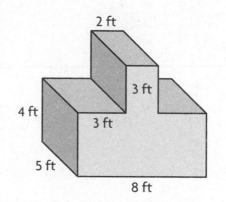

2 ft

3 ft

4 ft

3 ft

5 ft

8 ft

On Your Own

3 (MP) **Use Structure** Carlo is making a fabric chair filled with foam using the design shown. He wants to find the amount of foam he needs to make the chair.

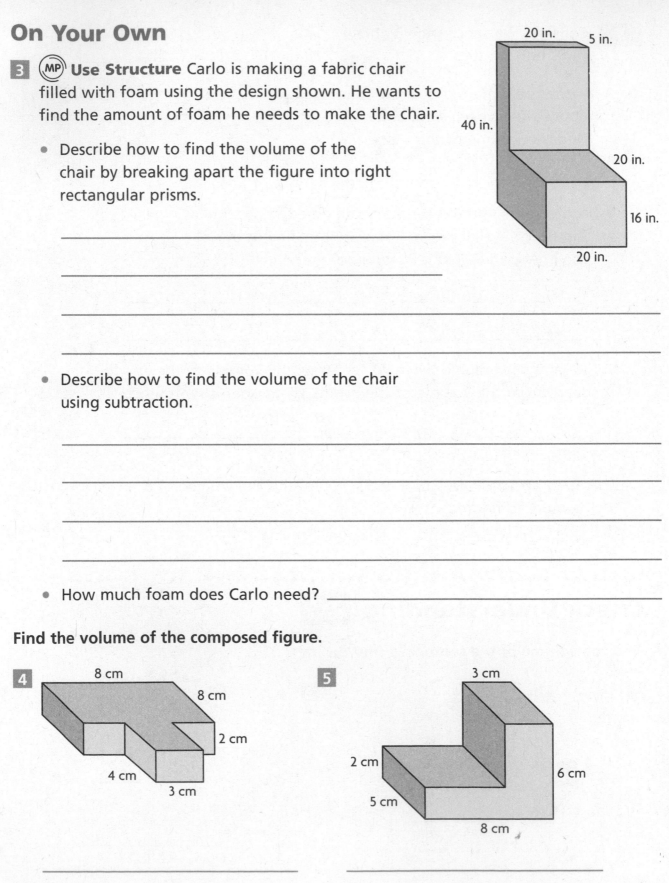

- Describe how to find the volume of the chair by breaking apart the figure into right rectangular prisms.

_____

_____

_____

_____

- Describe how to find the volume of the chair using subtraction.

_____

_____

_____

_____

- How much foam does Carlo need? _____

Find the volume of the composed figure.

4

5

6 (MP) **Reason** The volume of the composed figure shown is 88 cubic inches. What is the unknown number? Explain how you know.

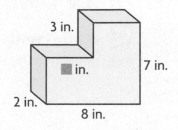

3 in.

▪ in.

7 in.

2 in.

8 in.

_____

_____

_____

Find the volume of the composed figure.

7

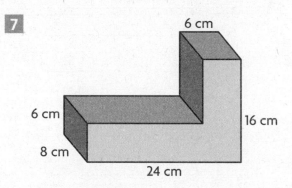

6 cm

6 cm

8 cm

16 cm

24 cm

_____

8

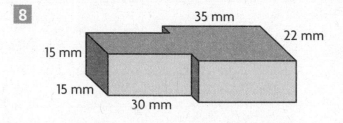

35 mm

22 mm

15 mm

15 mm

30 mm

_____

9

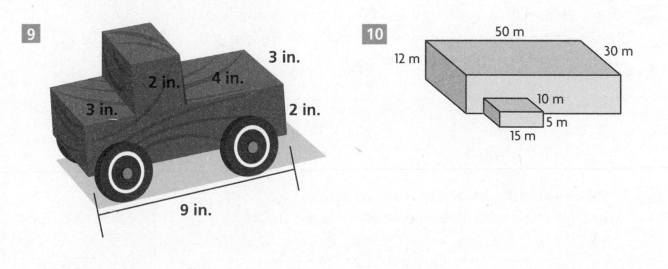

3 in.

2 in.

4 in.

3 in.

2 in.

9 in.

_____

10

50 m

30 m

12 m

10 m

5 m

15 m

_____

On Your Own

11 (MP) **Model with Mathematics** Write an addition expression to model the volume of the solid figure.

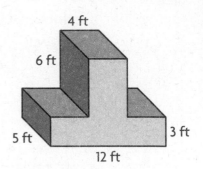

_____

Write the unknown dimensions, and then find the volume of the composed figure.

12

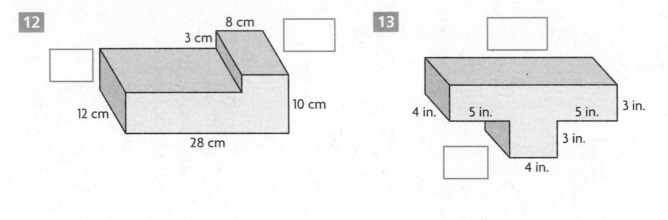

_____

13

_____

14 **Open Ended** Draw a composed figure with a volume of 36 cubic feet. Label the measurements of the figure, and show that the volume is 36 cubic feet.

15 (MP) **Model with Mathematics** Write a subtraction expression to model the volume of the solid figure.

_____

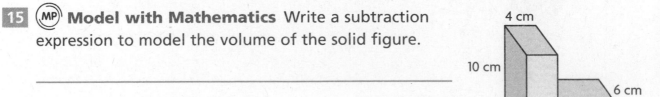

5 Review

Vocabulary

1 Draw lines to match the description to the term.

A solid figure that is 1 unit long,   •   • cubic units
1 unit wide, and 1 unit high

The units with which the space taken •   • unit cube
up by a solid object is measured

The measure of the space   •   • volume
a solid figure occupies

Concepts and Skills

2 **(MP) Use Tools** Find the number of unit cubes used to build the solid figure. Tell what strategy or tool you will use to answer the question, explain your choice, and then find the answer.

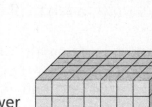

_____

_____

Use the unit given. Find the volume.

3

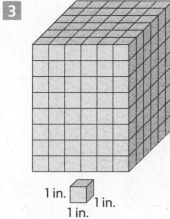

1 in. ☐ 1 in.
1 in.

4

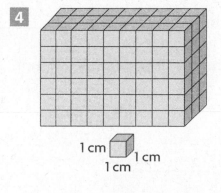

1 cm ☐ 1 cm
1 cm

_____   _____

5 The box is packed with jewelry boxes that have a volume of 4 cubic inches each. Select all the choices that describe the volume of the large box.

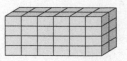

(A) 48 jewelry boxes

(D) 192 jewelry boxes

(B) 48 cubic units

(E) 192 cu in.

(C) 48 cu in.

(F) 192 cu ft

6 Select all the choices that describe a right rectangular prism with a volume equal to 240 cubic units.

(A) a cube with a side length of 6 units

(B) a base area of 20 square units and a height of 12 units

(C) a length of 5 units, a width of 6 units, and a height of 8 units

(D) contains exactly 16 smaller prisms with a volume of 15 cubic units each

(E) can be filled completely with 4 layers of 6 cubes with no gaps or overlaps

7 A truck hauls a trailer with a container in the shape of a right rectangular prism that is 40 feet long, 8 feet wide, and 9 feet high.

What is the volume of the container? _____

8 Gina stores 160 cubic inches of blocks in a container shaped like a right rectangular prism that has a base area of 36 square inches and a height of 5 inches. How much empty space remains in the container after

all of the blocks are put inside? _____

Find the volume of the composed figure.

9

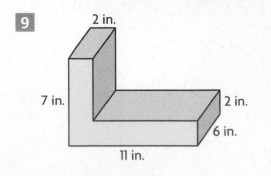

2 in.

7 in.

2 in.

6 in.

11 in.

10

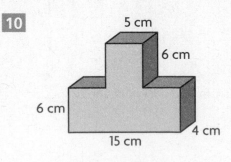

5 cm

6 cm

6 cm

15 cm

4 cm

_____   _____

Add and Subtract Fractions and Mixed Numbers

Fashion Designer

© Houghton Mifflin Harcourt Publishing Company • Image Credit: ©scyther5/iStock/Getty Images

Many fashion designers have an eye for design and detail. They make many types of clothing. Designers sketch their ideas, and they choose colors, patterns, and fabrics to complement the design. They also collaborate with others to make the products.

Many fashion designers in the United States work in New York and California.

To be a successful fashion designer, you need to have artistic, communication, and computer skills.

Fashion designers design accessories too—like handbags, ties, and shoes.

STEM Task:

Design a fabric pattern that you can describe using fractions such as "$\frac{1}{4}$ of the shapes are green," or "$\frac{1}{3}$ of the shapes are squares." Draw a simple shape, such as a leaf, on an index card. Carefully cut it out. Use the shape as a template and trace it multiple times on a sheet of paper. Make additional templates to add other shapes to your design. Color your design any way you choose.

Learning Mindset
Challenge-Seeking Defines Own Challenges

Believing in yourself is important, but so is making a plan and not giving up. Set realistic goals and know that the challenge may not be immediately achieved. By defining your own challenges, you can focus on the work that needs to be done to achieve your goals. Then you can find a new challenge. How did you challenge yourself when you made your fabric design? We often adjust challenges in tasks to keep them interesting. If a task is too easy, you can get bored. If it's too hard, you can get frustrated. Sometimes you need to adjust your work on a task to keep it engaging.

Reflect

Q Did you challenge yourself to come up with an interesting design?

Q What types of challenges interest you the most?

Understand Addition and Subtraction of Fractions with Unlike Denominators

WHAT FRACTION IS EACH PUZZLE PIECE?

- What fraction of the whole square does each puzzle piece represent?

Orange triangle: _____   Yellow triangle: _____

Light blue triangle: _____   Aqua square: _____

Green triangle: _____   Pink parallelogram: _____

Dark blue triangle: _____

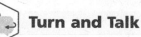

Turn and Talk

- How can you draw lines to help determine the fractions?

- Predict the sum of your fractions. Explain how you know.

- What two pieces can be used to represent $\frac{1}{2}$? Explain how you know.

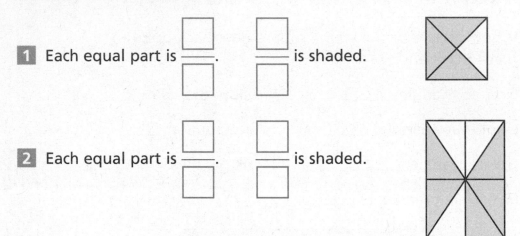

Are You Ready?

Complete these problems to review prior concepts and skills
you will need for this module.

Part of a Whole

Write the fraction that names the equal part. Then write a fraction to name the
shaded part of the whole.

1 Each equal part is $\frac{\boxed{}}{\boxed{}}$. $\frac{\boxed{}}{\boxed{}}$ is shaded.

2 Each equal part is $\frac{\boxed{}}{\boxed{}}$. $\frac{\boxed{}}{\boxed{}}$ is shaded.

Add and Subtract Fractions

Find the sum or difference.

3 $\frac{3}{8} + \frac{3}{8} =$ _____

4 $\frac{5}{9} - \frac{2}{9} =$ _____

5 $\frac{1}{6} + \frac{5}{6} =$ _____

6 $\frac{2}{5} + \frac{1}{5} =$ _____

7 $\frac{1}{3} + \frac{1}{3} =$ _____

8 $\frac{4}{7} - \frac{2}{7} =$ _____

9 $\frac{3}{4} - \frac{1}{4} =$ _____

10 $\frac{7}{8} - \frac{5}{8} =$ _____

11 $\frac{4}{9} + \frac{1}{9} =$ _____

Multiples

Write the first six nonzero multiples.

12 2 _____

13 9 _____

14 8 _____

15 4 _____

16 6 _____

17 3 _____

Name _____

Represent Fraction Sums and Differences

(I Can) make a visual model to represent the addition or subtraction of fractions with different-sized parts.

Spark Your Learning

Four hikers travel along the same trail over two days. The fraction of the trail each hiker travels is shown.

	Alexi	Rachel	James	Jayla
Day 1	$\frac{1}{2}$	$\frac{2}{5}$	$\frac{1}{2}$	$\frac{1}{2}$
Day 2	$\frac{1}{12}$	$\frac{1}{10}$	$\frac{1}{4}$	$\frac{3}{8}$

Use the data in the table to show two ways to represent the fraction of the trail one of the hikers travels on both days.

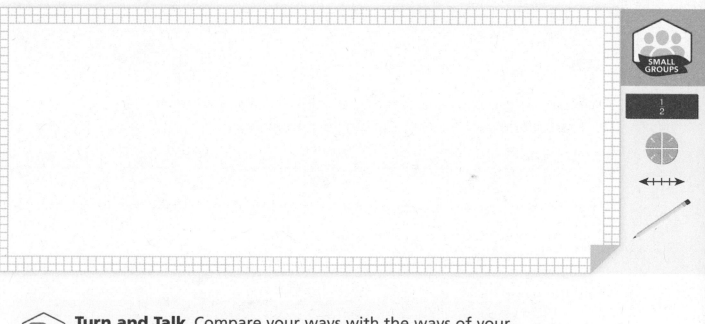

Turn and Talk Compare your ways with the ways of your classmates. How are they the same? How are they different?

Build Understanding

1 Marley and Jackie save together to buy a tent for their camping trip. Marley saves $\frac{3}{8}$ of the cost of the tent. Jackie saves $\frac{1}{2}$ of the cost of the tent. How much do Marley and Jackie save toward the cost of the tent?

How can you represent the situation? Draw to show your thinking.

A. How did you combine $\frac{3}{8}$ and $\frac{1}{2}$ to help you find how much Marley and Jackie save? Explain your thinking.

_____

_____

B. Write an equation to model your solution.

_____

 Turn and Talk How could you have solved this problem another way? Compare your answer with those of your classmates.

2 Pedro takes a $\frac{1}{2}$-pound bag of trail mix on his hike. During the hike, he eats $\frac{1}{4}$ pound of the trail mix. How much trail mix does he have left?

   A. How can you use fraction strips to represent the situation? Draw to show your thinking.

   B. What size fraction strip pieces can you use to represent the amount of trail mix he has left?

   _____

   C. Write an equation to model the amount of trail mix

   he has left. What is the amount? _____

 Turn and Talk Suppose Pedro has $\frac{3}{4}$ pound of trail mix at the start of the hike and he eats $\frac{1}{3}$ pound. How can you find the amount of trail mix he has left using fraction strips? How does this fraction model compare to the one you used in the problem above?

• •

Check Understanding [Math Board]

1 Claudia starts at the nature center and walks $\frac{1}{2}$ mile along a trail to this signpost. How far is the waterfall from the nature center?

waterfall $\frac{1}{12}$ mi

   • How can you use fraction strips to represent the distance from the nature center to the waterfall? Draw to show your thinking.

   • Write an equation to show the distance from the nature center to the waterfall. What is the distance?

_____

On Your Own

2 (MP) **Model with Mathematics** Luna hammers a stake into the ground for her tent. The stake is $\frac{7}{8}$ foot long. She hammers the stake $\frac{3}{4}$ foot into the ground.

- How long is the part of the stake that is above the ground? _____

- Draw to represent how you solved this problem.

- Write an equation to model the solution.

_____

3 (MP) **Use Tools** Tyler's cell phone has $\frac{7}{10}$ of its charge left at the start of his hike, and $\frac{1}{5}$ at the end.

- How much of the phone's charge is used

  during the hike? _____

- Draw to represent how you solved this problem.

4 (MP) **Reason** Why is it important to represent fractions with the same-sized parts when adding and subtracting?

_____

⊟✕ I'm in a Learning Mindset!
⊞÷

How did collaborating with a classmate help me make good decisions when representing fraction sums and differences?

_____

Name _____

Represent Addition with Different-Sized Parts

(I Can) represent the sum of fractions with different-sized parts using a visual model.

Spark Your Learning

Julia runs through an obstacle course. She climbs a cargo net in $\frac{1}{4}$ minute. Then she crosses the balance beam in $\frac{1}{6}$ minute. How long does Julia take to complete both obstacles?

Draw to show your reasoning.

PAIRS

$\frac{1}{2}$

How long does Julia take to complete both obstacles?

_____

 Turn and Talk As her final obstacle, Julia finishes the army crawl in $\frac{1}{2}$ minute. Does she finish the three obstacles in less than 1 minute? Explain.

Build Understanding

1 Some obstacle courses include a rope climb. On his first try, Travis climbs $\frac{2}{3}$ of the length of the rope. On his second try, he climbs more than his first try by $\frac{1}{6}$ of the length of rope. What part of the rope does Travis climb on his second try?

Complete the fraction model to solve the problem. Draw to show your thinking.

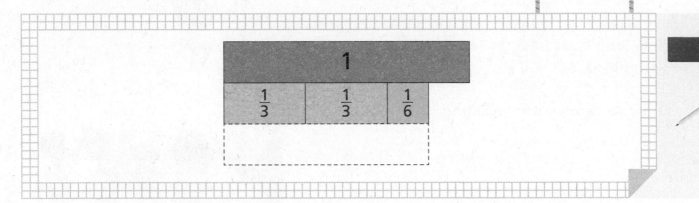

A. One student used all $\frac{1}{6}$-fraction strips to find the part of the rope Travis climbed on his second try. Another student used all $\frac{1}{12}$-fraction strips. Who is correct and how do you know?

_____

_____

B. Could you use only thirds to represent the sum? Explain.

_____

C. Write an equation to model your solution. _____

D. What part of the rope does Travis climb on his second try?

_____

 Turn and Talk A student solves this problem by looking at the fraction strip that was missing. What could this student have been thinking?

2 To make the obstacle course more challenging, the swinging rings are moved $\frac{1}{2}$ foot farther apart. If they were $\frac{5}{8}$ foot apart, how far apart are the rings now?

A. How does the new distance between the rings compare to the length of 1 foot?

_____

_____

B. Draw a visual model to represent the situation.

C. How far apart are the rings now? How do you know?

_____

Check Understanding Math Board

1 Jane buys a new pair of sneakers. The heel height of her old pair is $\frac{5}{6}$ inch. The heel height of her new pair is $\frac{1}{12}$ inch taller. What is the heel height of her new sneakers? Draw a visual model.

On Your Own

2 (MP) **Use Structure** Tina is making a vitamin drink to enjoy while training for an obstacle course. If she adds $\frac{1}{2}$ cup of water to the mix, how many cups of vitamin drink does Tina make? Draw a visual model that supports your answer.

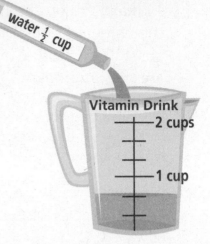

_____

(MP) **Use Tools** Use a visual model to find the sum.

3 $\frac{1}{4} + \frac{5}{6}$

4 $\frac{2}{3} + \frac{1}{6}$

5 $\frac{3}{10} + \frac{1}{2}$

_____   _____   _____

6 $\frac{3}{5} + \frac{1}{2}$

7 $\frac{1}{12} + \frac{5}{6}$

8 $\frac{3}{8} + \frac{3}{4}$

_____   _____   _____

9 **Open Ended** At the archery obstacle, Jasper's arrow lands $\frac{9}{10}$ inch from the center of the target. The distance from Jasper's arrow to the center of the target is $\frac{4}{5}$ inch less than the distance from Ali's arrow to the center of the target. Write a question based on this situation and then answer it.

_____

_____

⬡ I'm in a Learning Mindset!

How did collaborating with a partner support my learning about representing fractions with different-sized parts?

_____

Name _____

Represent Subtraction with Different-Sized Parts

(I Can) represent the difference between fractions with different-sized parts using a visual model.

Spark Your Learning

Mark and his friends are putting on a play. Mark is in charge of the costumes. He measures each sleeve in one costume to be $\frac{3}{4}$ yard long. Each sleeve should be $\frac{1}{2}$ yard long. By how much should each sleeve be shortened?

Draw a visual model to represent how much each sleeve should be shortened.

SMALL GROUPS

$\frac{1}{2}$

By how much should each sleeve be shortened? _____

Turn and Talk What part of the visual model shows how much each sleeve should be shortened? How do you know?

Build Understanding

1 Anderson and Joanne sold tickets for the play. Anderson sold $\frac{3}{4}$ of the roll of tickets, and Joanne sold $\frac{1}{6}$ of the roll of tickets.

What is the difference between the fractions of the roll of tickets that Anderson and Joanne sold?

A. Explain what the dashed box in the fraction model represents.

1		
$\frac{1}{4}$	$\frac{1}{4}$	$\frac{1}{4}$
$\frac{1}{6}$		

_____

B. Who sold more tickets? How do you know?

_____

C. Use the fraction model in Part A to draw fraction strips in the dashed box to solve the problem. What size fraction strips did you draw? Explain.

_____

_____

D. What is the difference between the fractions of the roll of tickets that Anderson and Joanne sold?

_____

 Turn and Talk How could you represent this problem using only $\frac{1}{12}$-fraction strips?

2 Two boxes have the same number of play programs. On the first night of the play, Diana handed out $\frac{2}{3}$ of a box. On the second night, she handed out $\frac{5}{12}$ of the other box. On which night did Diana hand out more programs? How much more of a fractional part of a box did she hand out?

Draw a visual model to represent the situation.

A. On which night did she hand out more programs? How do you know?

_____

_____

B. How much more of a fractional part of a box did she hand out? How does your visual model show this?

_____

_____

Check Understanding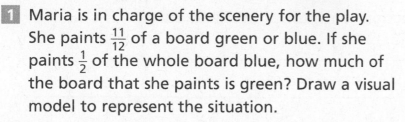

1 Maria is in charge of the scenery for the play. She paints $\frac{11}{12}$ of a board green or blue. If she paints $\frac{1}{2}$ of the whole board blue, how much of the board that she paints is green? Draw a visual model to represent the situation.

On Your Own

2 (MP) **Use Structure** Greta and Tran have the lead roles in the play. Greta is on stage for $\frac{3}{4}$ of the play. Tran is on stage for $\frac{2}{3}$ of the play. What is the difference between the fractions of the play that Greta and Tran each spend on stage? Draw a visual model to represent the difference.

_____

(MP) **Use Tools** Use a visual model to find the difference.

3 $\frac{11}{12} - \frac{2}{3} =$ _____

4 $\frac{3}{5} - \frac{3}{10}$ _____

5 $\frac{9}{8} - \frac{1}{4} =$ _____

6 Hannah prints t-shirts for everyone working on the play. Her printing machine uses $\frac{1}{2}$ milliliter of ink for each shirt. The front of each shirt uses $\frac{2}{5}$ milliliter of ink. How much ink does the printer use for the back of each shirt?

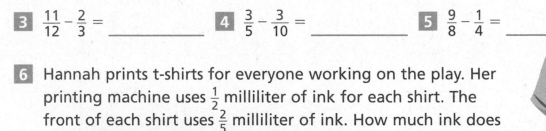

_____

✚✖️✕ I'm in a Learning Mindset!

What would I like to learn more about when I am studying how to use visual models to subtract fractions with different-sized parts?

_____

_____

Name _____

Rewrite Fractions with a Common Denominator

(I Can) generate equivalent fractions for given fractions using a common denominator.

Spark Your Learning

TV show hosts Ben and Isa are preparing small pieces of French toast from slices of bread. Ben cuts his slice into two equal sections. Isa cuts her slice into three equal sections. All of the sections were supposed to be cut into the same-sized pieces.

Draw a visual model to show what Ben and Isa should do to correct the sizes of their sections of French toast.

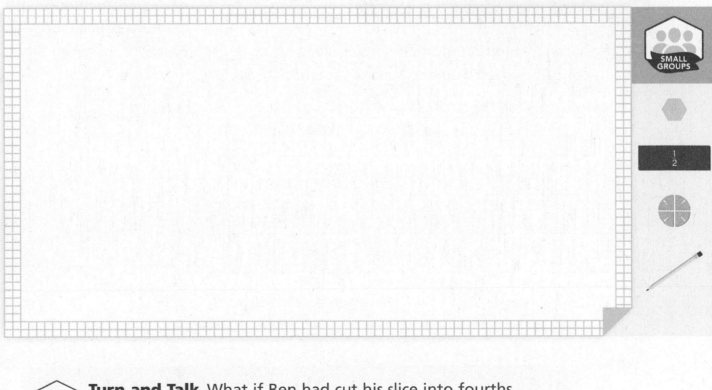

Turn and Talk What if Ben had cut his slice into fourths instead of halves? What would Ben and Isa need to do then?

Build Understanding

1 The circle represents all the people who watch *The Morning Show*. What equivalent fractions can you write to represent the different ways people watch *The Morning Show*?

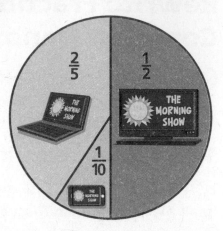

A. List nonzero multiples of 2, 5, and 10.

2: _____

5: _____

10: _____

B. What is a common multiple of 2, 5, and 10?

_____

C. Use the common multiple you found to write equivalent fractions.

$\frac{1}{2}$ = _____ $\frac{2}{5}$ = _____ $\frac{1}{10}$ = _____

D. How can a common multiple and equivalent fractions help you add and subtract fractions?

_____

_____

_____

_____

_____

> **Connect to Vocabulary**
>
> Fractions that name the same amount or part are **equivalent fractions**. For example, $\frac{1}{3}$ and $\frac{2}{6}$ are equivalent fractions.

E. Write a numerical expression using equivalent fractions that models all the people who watch *The Morning Show*.

_____

Turn and Talk How do you know how many multiples to list when you are finding a common multiple of 2, 5, and 10?

142

Step It Out

2 Trina makes decorations using wire. She has one piece of wire that is $\frac{1}{6}$ foot and another piece that is $\frac{3}{4}$ foot. What equivalent fractions represent the amounts of wire that Trina has?

A. Find the product of the denominators of each fraction. How is your answer related to the common multiples of 4 and 6?

_____

B. What equivalent fractions with a common denominator can you write for $\frac{3}{4}$ and $\frac{1}{6}$?

_____

C. What numerical expression using equivalent fractions models the amount of wire that Trina has?

_____

> **Connect to Vocabulary**
>
> A **common denominator** is a common multiple of two or more denominators. Any two or more fractions can be expressed as equivalent fractions with a common denominator.

• •

Check Understanding [Math Board]

1 Ava, Kate, and Jin bring all the food to a picnic. Ava brings $\frac{3}{4}$, Kate brings $\frac{1}{6}$, and Jin brings $\frac{1}{12}$. Write a numerical expression using equivalent fractions with a common denominator to model the amounts of food they bring to the picnic.

_____

Find a common denominator. Then use the common denominator to write equivalent fractions.

2 $\frac{3}{4}, \frac{1}{8}$

Common denominator: _____

_____

3 $\frac{1}{4}, \frac{5}{6}$

Common denominator: _____

_____

On Your Own

4 (MP) **Reason** *The Morning Show* has a $\frac{1}{5}$-hour weather section and a $\frac{1}{2}$-hour news section. How can you determine the amount of time spent on weather and news without using drawings?

_____

_____

_____

Use a common denominator to write equivalent fractions.

5 $\frac{1}{2}, \frac{5}{12}$

_____

6 $\frac{2}{3}, \frac{1}{6}$

_____

7 $\frac{2}{3}, \frac{3}{8}$

_____

8 $\frac{1}{4}, \frac{3}{5}$

_____

9 $\frac{3}{4}, \frac{1}{6}$

_____

10 $\frac{2}{3}, \frac{3}{5}$

_____

11 **STEM** Temperature is one factor that determines the weather. In Tavernier, Florida, the average monthly high temperature (°F) is in the 70s for $\frac{1}{3}$ of the year, in the 80s for $\frac{1}{2}$ of the year, and in the 90s for $\frac{1}{6}$ of the year. Write a numerical expression using equivalent fractions with a common denominator to model the part of the year with these average temperatures.

_____

➗ I'm in a Learning Mindset!

How do I break down finding a common denominator into smaller steps?

_____

_____

Review

Vocabulary

1 Draw lines to match the example to the term.

For the fraction $\frac{2}{5}$, an •
example of this is $\frac{4}{10}$.
                                        • common denominator

For the fraction $\frac{3}{8}$, the •
number 8 represents this.
                                        • equivalent fraction

For the fractions $\frac{1}{6}$ and $\frac{2}{3}$, •
an example of this is 18.
                                        • equal parts in the whole

Concepts and Skills

2 **(MP)** **Use Tools** Select all numbers that can be used as a common
denominator to write equivalent fractions for $\frac{1}{2}$ and $\frac{5}{6}$. Name the
strategy or tool you will use to solve the problem, explain your
choice, and then find the answer.

(A) 2   (C) 6   (E) 12

(B) 4   (D) 8   (F) 18

_____

_____

Use a common denominator to write equivalent fractions.

3 $\frac{1}{10}, \frac{2}{5}$

4 $\frac{1}{3}, \frac{2}{5}$

5 $\frac{1}{4}, \frac{2}{6}$

6 $\frac{2}{3}, \frac{5}{9}$

7 Mikaela decorates a cake. When she starts, $\frac{5}{6}$ of the tube has decorative icing. She uses $\frac{3}{4}$ of the tube to decorate the cake. What fraction of the tube is left? Draw a visual model.

_____

8 Amy eats $\frac{1}{3}$ of a small pizza at a restaurant and takes the rest home. The next day, Amy eats $\frac{1}{4}$ of the pizza for lunch. What fraction of the pizza has Amy eaten? Draw a visual model.

_____

9 Declan has $\frac{1}{2}$ pound of turkey. He eats $\frac{1}{3}$ pound for lunch. Which fraction strips represent the amount of turkey he has left?

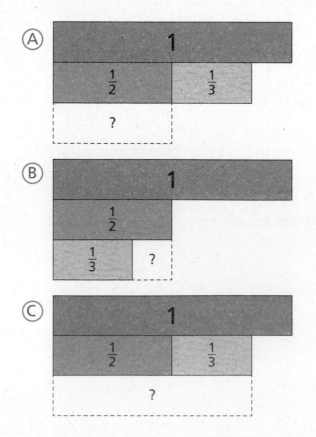

Add and Subtract Fractions and Mixed Numbers with Unlike Denominators

Can you place the numbers?

- Use each of the numbers on the cards to write an equation using mixed numbers with like denominators.

Turn and Talk

- How did you solve the problem?

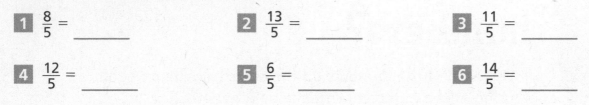
Are You Ready?

Complete these problems to review prior concepts and skills you will need for this module.

Explore Mixed Numbers

Write the fraction as a mixed number.

1 $\frac{8}{5}$ = _____

2 $\frac{13}{5}$ = _____

3 $\frac{11}{5}$ = _____

4 $\frac{12}{5}$ = _____

5 $\frac{6}{5}$ = _____

6 $\frac{14}{5}$ = _____

Equivalent Fractions

Complete the equation to show how the two fractions are equivalent.

7

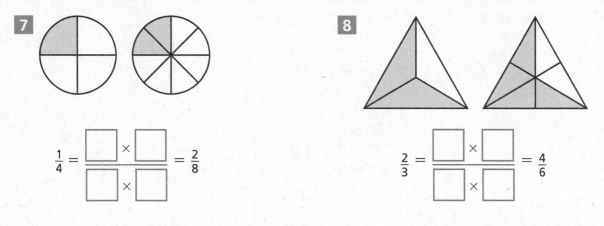

$$\frac{1}{4} = \frac{\boxed{} \times \boxed{}}{\boxed{} \times \boxed{}} = \frac{2}{8}$$

8

$$\frac{2}{3} = \frac{\boxed{} \times \boxed{}}{\boxed{} \times \boxed{}} = \frac{4}{6}$$

Add and Subtract Fractions

Find the sum or difference.

9 $\frac{2}{8} + \frac{5}{8}$ = _____

10 $\frac{7}{9} - \frac{1}{9}$ = _____

11 $\frac{1}{6} + \frac{1}{6}$ = _____

12 $\frac{1}{5} + \frac{2}{5}$ = _____

13 $\frac{2}{3} + \frac{1}{3}$ = _____

14 $\frac{6}{7} - \frac{1}{7}$ = _____

15 $\frac{7}{9} - \frac{2}{9}$ = _____

16 $\frac{7}{8} - \frac{3}{8}$ = _____

17 $\frac{1}{4} + \frac{1}{4}$ = _____

Name _____

Use Benchmarks and Number Sense to Estimate

(I Can) use benchmarks to estimate a sum or difference of fractions with unlike denominators.

Spark Your Learning

Ms. Fong mixes water, glue, and laundry detergent together to make slime. The amount of each ingredient is a fraction of a liter.

Use a visual model to estimate the total number of liters of ingredients she mixes together.

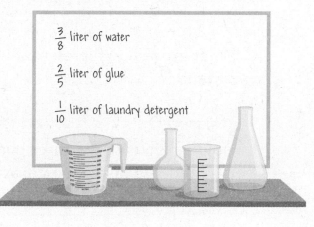

$\frac{3}{8}$ liter of water

$\frac{2}{5}$ liter of glue

$\frac{1}{10}$ liter of laundry detergent

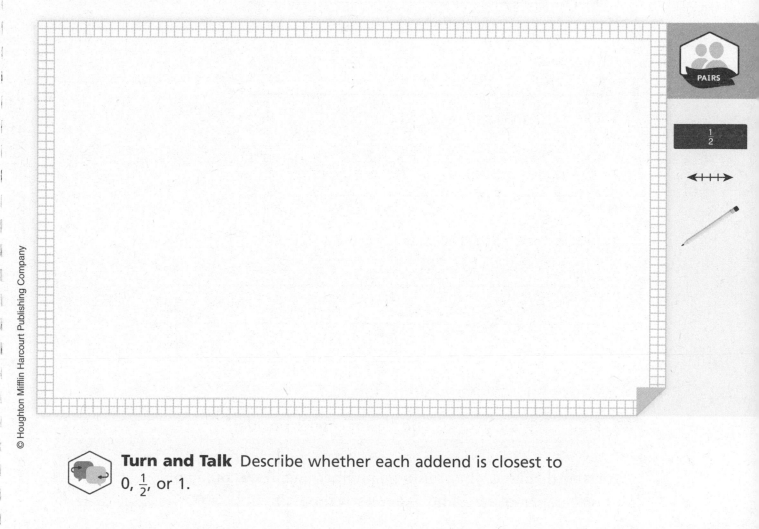

PAIRS

$\frac{1}{2}$

Turn and Talk Describe whether each addend is closest to 0, $\frac{1}{2}$, or 1.

Build Understanding

1 Ms. Fong has some bottles of copper powder for science experiments. She uses $\frac{7}{8}$ bottle, $\frac{2}{3}$ bottle, and $\frac{5}{12}$ bottle. About how many bottles of copper powder does she use?

A. What expression represents the situation?

_____

B. How can you use the three number lines and the **benchmarks** 0, $\frac{1}{2}$, and 1 to help you estimate the answer?

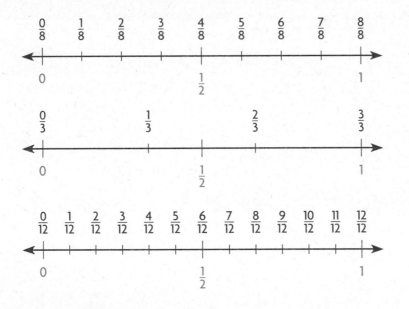

_____

_____

_____

C. What expression represents the estimate? _____

Ms. Fong uses about _____ bottles of copper powder.

  Turn and Talk Without using a number line, how could you determine whether $\frac{7}{8}$ and $\frac{5}{12}$ are each closest to 0, $\frac{1}{2}$, or 1?

Step It Out

2 Each group in science class has a 2-liter container of distilled water. Group A uses $1\frac{9}{10}$ L and Group B uses $1\frac{3}{8}$ L. About how much more distilled water does Group A use than Group B?

A. Represent the situation with an expression. _____

B. Determine an estimate without finding an exact answer.

- Between which two whole numbers does $1\frac{9}{10}$ lie? _____

- Is the fractional part of the mixed number closest to 0, $\frac{1}{2}$, or 1? Explain.

  _____

  _____

- What whole number can you use to estimate $1\frac{9}{10}$? _____

- Use benchmark values to estimate $1\frac{3}{8}$. _____

- Write an equation to estimate the difference.

  _____

C. About how much more distilled water does Group A use than Group B?

  _____

• •

Check Understanding [Math Board]

1 A weather station reports that $\frac{11}{12}$ foot of snow fell yesterday afternoon and $\frac{1}{3}$ foot fell yesterday evening. Estimate the amount of snow that fell yesterday. _____

Use benchmark values to write an expression to represent an estimate.

2 $\frac{9}{10} + \frac{1}{12}$

3 $\frac{5}{8} - \frac{3}{5}$

On Your Own

4 **History** In the 1800s, wagon trains traveled west along the Oregon Trail. A wagon train traveled from Missouri to Wyoming in $1\frac{2}{3}$ months, and from Wyoming to Utah in $\frac{3}{5}$ month. About how many months did it take the wagon train to travel from Missouri to Utah?

_____

Use benchmarks to estimate the sum or difference.

5 $1\frac{5}{12} - \frac{2}{3}$ _____

6 $\frac{7}{10} + \frac{7}{8}$ _____

7 **(MP) Use Tools** Use the number lines and benchmarks to estimate $1\frac{1}{3} - \frac{5}{6}$.

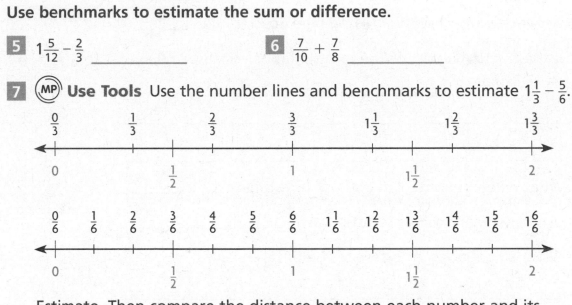

Estimate. Then compare the distance between each number and its benchmark. What does this tell you about the actual difference?

_____

_____

8 **Open Ended** Use mixed numbers or fractions with unlike denominators to write an addition expression and a subtraction expression, each with an estimate of $1\frac{1}{2}$. Justify your answer.

_____

© Houghton Mifflin Harcourt Publishing Company

⚙ I'm in a Learning Mindset!

Are the visual models effective in solving the problem?

_____

Name _____

Assess Reasonableness of Fraction Sums and Differences

(I Can) add and subtract fractions with unlike denominators using a common denominator and assess reasonableness.

Step It Out

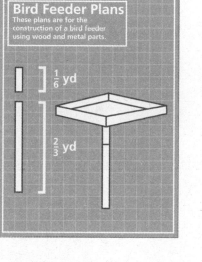

Bird Feeder Plans
These plans are for the construction of a bird feeder using wood and metal parts.

$\frac{1}{6}$ yd

$\frac{2}{3}$ yd

1 Jaime is building a bird feeder. He connects two metal rods together to make a stand. The blueprint for the project shows the lengths of the rods. What is the total length of the rods?

A. Write an expression to model the situation.

_____

B. Find a **common denominator** for the fractions in this expression.

_____

C. Write **equivalent fractions** using the common denominator.

_____

D. Write an expression using fractions with a common denominator. Then find the total length of the rods.

_____

E. Explain how you know your answer is reasonable.

_____

_____

 Turn and Talk Jon says you have to rewrite fractions with common denominators before you can estimate. Sarah says you can estimate without finding a common denominator first. Who do you think is correct and why?

Step It Out

2 Jaime fastens the bottom of the bird feeder to the pole. He has four boards that are each $\frac{5}{6}$-foot long. How much must Jaime cut from each board to make each side of the feeder $\frac{3}{4}$-foot long?

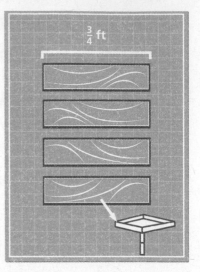

$\frac{3}{4}$ ft

A. Write an expression you can use to solve

the problem. _____

B. Write an expression using fractions with a common denominator to model the problem. Then find how much Jaime must cut from each board.

_____

C. Explain how you know your answer is reasonable.

_____

 Turn and Talk Look at the denominators of the given fractions. Note that neither denominator is a multiple of the other. How does this indicate that both fractions need to be renamed for them to have a common denominator?

....

Check Understanding [Math Board]

1 Jaime starts with $\frac{7}{8}$ ounce of glue. After a project, $\frac{1}{4}$ ounce of glue is left. Write an expression that can be used to find how much glue Jaime uses. Solve the problem. Show that your answer is reasonable.

_____

_____

Write the expression using fractions with a common denominator. Then find the sum or difference.

2 $\frac{2}{3} - \frac{1}{5}$ _____

3 $\frac{1}{6} + \frac{3}{4}$ _____

On Your Own

4 (MP) **Critique Reasoning** Kyle is stringing a necklace with beads. He puts black beads on $\frac{5}{8}$ of the string and white beads on $\frac{1}{4}$ of the string. Kyle thinks that he will cover $\frac{6}{12}$ of the string with beads. Is Kyle's claim reasonable?

_____

5 **STEM** Precipitation can be in the form of rain, snow, sleet, or hail. In Sarasota, Florida, it rains about $\frac{2}{3}$ inch on May 22 and about $\frac{5}{12}$ inch on May 25.

- What expression represents the difference in the amount of rainfall for the two days?

_____

- Write an expression using fractions with a common

  denominator. Then find the difference. _____

Write the expression using fractions with a common denominator. Then find the sum or difference.

6 $\frac{3}{8} + \frac{1}{6}$

_____

7 $\frac{3}{4} - \frac{7}{12}$

_____

8 $\frac{1}{6} + \frac{3}{9}$

_____

9 $\frac{7}{9} - \frac{1}{3}$

_____

10 Mr. Singh's laptop memory is $\frac{9}{10}$ full. After he deletes some files, the memory is $\frac{3}{5}$ full.

- What fraction represents the part of the laptop

  memory that he deletes? _____

- Is your answer reasonable? How do you know?

_____

_____

11 Tracy checks the digital tablets made at a factory. In one box of tablets, she finds that $\frac{1}{20}$ have a cracked screen. In the same box, she finds that another $\frac{1}{5}$ have the wrong software. What fraction of the tablets in the box have either a cracked screen or the wrong software?

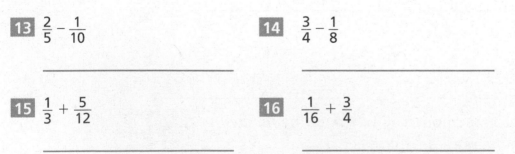

_____

12 (MP) **Use Structure** On Tuesday, the dance team spends $\frac{1}{8}$ of the practice time trying on uniforms and $\frac{1}{6}$ of the time choosing music. They spend the remaining time dancing.

- What fraction of practice time do they spend dancing?

_____

- Explain how you found your answer.

_____

_____

_____

Find the sum or difference.

13 $\frac{2}{5} - \frac{1}{10}$

_____

14 $\frac{3}{4} - \frac{1}{8}$

_____

15 $\frac{1}{3} + \frac{5}{12}$

_____

16 $\frac{1}{16} + \frac{3}{4}$

_____

17 (MP) **Attend to Precision** Malcolm completes $\frac{1}{5}$ of his new video game. After one week, he completes another $\frac{1}{10}$ of the game. After two weeks, he completes another $\frac{1}{2}$ of the game. How much of the game does he complete? Model with an expression and find the sum.

_____

Name

Assess Reasonableness of Mixed Number Sums and Differences

(I Can) add and subtract mixed numbers with unlike denominators and assess reasonableness.

Step It Out

1 Caroline trains every weekend for a track and field competition. She writes down how long she spends running sprints and jumping hurdles. How many hours does she spend training on Sunday?

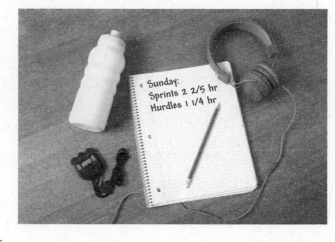

Sunday:
Sprints 2 2/5 hr
Hurdles 1 1/4 hr

A. Write an expression to model the situation.

_____

B. Estimate the answer.

_____

C. Rewrite the expression in Part A using equivalent fractions with a common denominator. Then find the sum.

_____

D. How many hours does Caroline spend training on Sunday?

_____

E. Is your answer reasonable? Explain.

_____

_____

 Turn and Talk Describe how to find the sum of two mixed numbers. How can you determine if the answer is reasonable?

Step It Out

2 Jonah's best pole vault jump is $7\frac{1}{4}$ feet. A sign in the gymnasium shows the gym's record. How much shorter than the gym's record is Jonah's best jump?

Pole Vault Record: $8\frac{7}{12}$ feet

A. Write an expression to model the situation.

_____

B. Estimate the answer. _____

C. Rewrite the expression in Part A using equivalent fractions

with a common denominator. _____

D. How far is Jonah's jump from the gym's record? Is your answer reasonable? Explain.

_____

_____

Turn and Talk If you first expressed each of these mixed numbers as a fraction greater than 1, how would your method change?

Check Understanding [Math Board]

1 Jenna competes in the high jump. Her best jump in the first meet is $4\frac{1}{4}$ feet. Her best jump in the second meet is $4\frac{5}{6}$ feet. Write an expression using equivalent fractions with a common denominator to model how much the height of her jump increases. By how much does the height of her jump increase? Show that your answer is reasonable.

_____

Write the expression using equivalent fractions with a common denominator. Then find the sum or difference.

2 $2\frac{3}{5} + 1\frac{3}{10}$

3 $3\frac{7}{8} - 1\frac{1}{2}$

_____   _____

On Your Own

4 Donna trains for a triathlon. Her fastest times for the three parts of the event are: swimming ($1\frac{1}{4}$ hr), running ($1\frac{1}{2}$ hr), and biking ($1\frac{1}{5}$ hr). If she matches her best times in all three parts, how long will it take her to finish the triathlon?

_____

5 (MP) **Attend to Precision** Richie estimates $1\frac{7}{8} - 1\frac{1}{6}$ to be about 1, but he finds the actual difference to be less than 1. Did he make a mistake? Explain.

_____

_____

_____

Find the sum or difference.

6 $3\frac{5}{6} - 1\frac{7}{12}$

7 $4\frac{1}{2} - 2\frac{1}{3}$

_____

8 $5\frac{1}{3} + 3\frac{3}{7}$

9 $2\frac{4}{9} + 1\frac{1}{4}$

_____

10 (MP) **Model with Mathematics** Shaia buys a bag of apples that weighs $2\frac{7}{16}$ pounds, and another bag that weighs $2\frac{1}{2}$ pounds.

- Estimate the weight of both bags of apples. Then find the exact weight.

_____

- Shaia also buys a bag of oranges that weighs $3\frac{5}{8}$ pounds. Write an expression to model how much more the bags of apples weigh than the bag of oranges. Then find the number of pounds.

_____

On Your Own

11 A restaurant's refrigerator contains $4\frac{1}{2}$ heads of lettuce. Marlon uses $3\frac{1}{4}$ of them to make a salad. How many heads of lettuce are left in the refrigerator?

_____

12 **Model with Mathematics** Ed buys a plant that will grow to be $8\frac{1}{2}$ inches tall. The plant Ed buys today is $3\frac{3}{8}$ inches tall.

- Write an expression using equivalent fractions with a common denominator to model how many more inches the plant is expected to grow. Then find the number of inches.

_____

- Addition and subtraction are inverse operations. How can you use inverse operations to check your answer?

_____

_____

13 **Open Ended** Jae makes a $10\frac{1}{6}$-foot path in two sections. Write an expression using two mixed numbers with unlike denominators that shows one way Jae can make the path in two sections. What is the length of each section?

_____

14 Abigail works $6\frac{1}{2}$ hours, $2\frac{2}{3}$ hours, and $4\frac{1}{4}$ hours this week. How many more hours will Abigail need to work this week to reach her goal of $18\frac{1}{2}$ hours?

_____

15 **Attend to Precision** For his daily exercise, Kado likes to travel 8 miles. Today he jogs $3\frac{2}{5}$ miles and walks $4\frac{7}{10}$ miles. Does Kado meet his goal? Explain.

_____

_____

Name _____

Rename Mixed Numbers to Subtract

(I Can) subtract mixed numbers by renaming.

Step It Out

1 ▶ Larry rides his bike to the park. On his way home, he gets a flat tire. How far does Larry have to walk his bike to get home?

(map shows: Home, $3\frac{1}{4}$ mi, Larry's flat tire, $2\frac{3}{8}$ mi, Park)

A. Write an expression for the problem.

_____

B. Use fraction strips to represent the distance Larry rode to the park as an equivalent fraction with a denominator of 8. Then

write a new subtraction expression. _____

C. Do you have enough fraction strips to subtract the fractional part of the distance Larry rode home? Explain.

_____

_____

D. How can you represent the distance Larry rode to the park using fraction strips so that you are able to subtract the distance Larry rode home before he got a flat tire?

_____

_____

E. Represent the exchange you made with the fraction strips using mixed numbers with an equation and subtract.

_____

F. How far does Larry walk his bike home? _____

 Turn and Talk How else could you rewrite the mixed numbers $3\frac{1}{4}$ and $2\frac{3}{8}$ so you can subtract $2\frac{3}{8}$? Explain your reasoning.

Step It Out

2 The students in a fifth-grade class and a fourth-grade class ate some pizza. How many more pizzas did the fifth-graders eat than the fourth-graders?

Pizza Eaten by the Fourth-Grade Class

A. Write an expression to model the problem.

_____

B. Estimate the answer. _____

C. Find a common denominator. Use the common denominator to write mixed numbers with equivalent fractions.

_____

D. You can subtract mixed numbers by renaming both numbers as fractions greater than 1. Rename each mixed number.

_____

E. Find the difference. Then rename the difference as a mixed number.

_____

F. How many more pizzas did the fifth-graders eat than the fourth-graders?

_____

G. Is your answer reasonable? Explain.

_____

_____

Turn and Talk Compare and contrast the method for renaming mixed numbers in this task and the task on the previous page. Which method do you prefer to use? Explain.

Name _____

3 Sarah measures how much water her horse and donkey each drink. How much more water does the horse drink than the donkey?

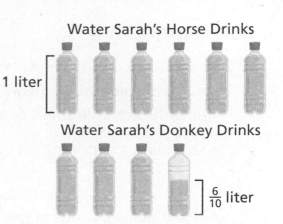

Water Sarah's Horse Drinks

1 liter

Water Sarah's Donkey Drinks

$\frac{6}{10}$ liter

A. What expression can you write to model the problem?

_____

B. Can you subtract the fractional part from the whole number? Explain.

_____

_____

_____

C. Rename the whole number to subtract and explain the process you use.

_____

_____

D. Find the difference. _____

E. How much more water does the horse drink than the donkey?

_____

• •

Check Understanding 🔲 Math Board

1 Marcus has a board that is $7\frac{1}{4}$ feet long. If he cuts off a piece that is $2\frac{1}{2}$ feet long, how long will the board be?

_____

Estimate. Then find the difference.

2 $4\frac{1}{3} - 2\frac{5}{6}$ _____

3 $5\frac{1}{4} - 1\frac{1}{3}$ _____

On Your Own

4 (MP) **Reason** Bethany has $3\frac{3}{8}$ pounds of peanuts in a bag. She feeds some of the peanuts to squirrels. How many pounds of peanuts does Bethany feed to the squirrels?

PEANUTS

$1\frac{13}{16}$ lb

After
Feeding Squirrels

- Estimate the difference.

  _____

- How many pounds of peanuts does she feed to the squirrels?

  _____

- Is your answer reasonable? Explain.

  _____

Estimate. Then find the difference.

5 $5\frac{1}{3} - 1\frac{7}{8}$

6 $3\frac{1}{4} - 2\frac{4}{5}$

7 $6\frac{1}{2} - 4\frac{9}{10}$

8 $8\frac{1}{3} - 2\frac{5}{6}$

9 $9\frac{3}{8} - 3\frac{1}{2}$

10 $11 - 8\frac{1}{12}$

11 Franco practices the piano for $4\frac{1}{2}$ hours each week. He plays soccer for $1\frac{3}{4}$ hours. How much longer does Franco practice piano than play soccer?

_____

12 Hannah grows two corn plants. The first plant is $6\frac{1}{4}$ feet tall. The second plant is $4\frac{6}{8}$ feet tall. How much taller is the first corn plant?

_____

© Houghton Mifflin Harcourt Publishing Company

13 (MP) **Critique Reasoning** Cata walks the long way to school. On her way home, she takes a shortcut. Cata says the shortcut saves at least 1 mile. Is Cata's reasoning correct? Explain.

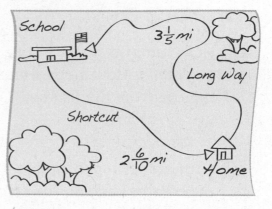

_____

_____

_____

14 (MP) **Model with Mathematics** Thomas watched two movies this weekend. _Cenozoic World_ lasted $2\frac{1}{6}$ hours. _Happy Robots_ lasted $1\frac{3}{4}$ hours. How many hours longer was _Cenozoic World_ than _Happy Robots_? Write an expression to model the problem. Then solve.

_____

Estimate. Then find the difference.

15 $4\frac{1}{3} - 2\frac{4}{5}$

16 $3\frac{1}{3} - 1\frac{6}{9}$

_____

17 $10 - 5\frac{7}{8}$

18 $6\frac{1}{3} - 3\frac{2}{4}$

_____

19 $8\frac{2}{3} - 3\frac{11}{12}$

20 $16 - 7\frac{5}{12}$

_____

21 Keshawn runs $6\frac{3}{8}$ laps around a track. Mark runs $3\frac{3}{4}$ laps around the track. How many more laps does Keshawn run than Mark?

_____

22 Ryan rakes leaves for 3 hours. The time he spends raking leaves is $1\frac{1}{4}$ hours more than the time he spends playing basketball. How long does Ryan play basketball?

_____

On Your Own

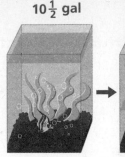
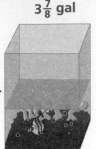

$10\frac{1}{2}$ gal $3\frac{7}{8}$ gal

23 Holly removes water from a fish tank to clean it. How much water does Holly remove from the fish tank?

_____

24 Fifth-grade students plant a class garden. They plant $7\frac{1}{6}$ rows of tomatoes and $3\frac{1}{2}$ rows of carrots. How many fewer rows of carrots than rows of tomatoes do the students plant?

_____

25 (MP) **Model with Mathematics** Jae needs $4\frac{1}{4}$ cups of flour to make two pizzas for dinner. He has $2\frac{1}{2}$ cups of flour. How many more cups of flour does he need? Write an expression to model the problem. Then solve.

_____

26 (MP) **Reason** A weather balloon is $3\frac{1}{10}$ miles above the ground. Later, it is $1\frac{3}{5}$ miles above the ground.

- How far did the balloon descend?

_____

- How do you know your answer is reasonable?

_____

_____

27 (MP) **Construct Arguments** Ms. Hendricks buys $4\frac{1}{4}$ yards of fabric. She uses $2\frac{1}{2}$ yards of the fabric to make a curtain. She needs $1\frac{3}{4}$ yards of fabric to cover a footrest. Does Ms. Hendricks have enough fabric to cover the footrest? Explain.

_____

_____

Apply Properties of Addition

(I Can) apply the properties of addition to add fractions and mixed numbers.

Step It Out

EXPERIENCE LEVEL

1 As Pria plays a computer game, the experience bar fills to show her experience level. The bar fills to $\frac{1}{5}$ before completing a level. After completing the level, the bar fills another $\frac{3}{5}$. As a bonus, it fills an additional $\frac{1}{10}$. What is her experience level now?

A. Write an addition expression to model the situation.

$\frac{1}{5} + ($ _____ + _____ $)$

B. Based on the expression you wrote in Part A, how can you use the **Commutative Property of Addition**, the **Associative Property of Addition**, or both properties to help you find the sum?

_____

_____

C. Use the properties of addition to group the fractions with like denominators together.

_____ + _____

D. Find the sum of the fractions in the parentheses.

_____ + _____

E. Write equivalent fractions with like denominators.

_____ + _____

F. Find the sum.

_____

What is Pria's experience level now?

_____

Turn and Talk How can you estimate to show the sum is reasonable, without evaluating the expression?

Step It Out

2 Add. $1\frac{5}{9} + 3\frac{5}{6} + 1\frac{2}{9}$

A. Use the Commutative Property of Addition to put fractions with the same denominator next to each other.

_____

B. Use the Associative Property of Addition and parentheses to group fractions with like denominators together.

_____

C. Add the terms located inside the parentheses.

_____

D. Write equivalent fractions with like denominators.

_____

E. Find the sum. Rename if needed.

_____

Turn and Talk How are the properties of addition helpful for finding sums of expressions that have three or more addends?

Check Understanding [Math Board]

1 Michael plans to hike from the ranger station to the mountain top. The map shows the lengths of the different parts of the trail. What is the distance, in miles, from the station to the mountain top?

_____

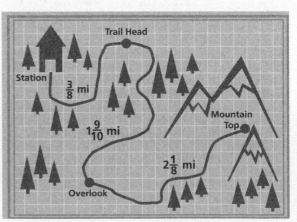

Add.

2 $\frac{3}{5} + \left(\frac{1}{2} + \frac{4}{5}\right)$

3 $\left(1\frac{1}{4} + 1\frac{2}{3}\right) + 2\frac{2}{3}$

4 $2\frac{5}{8} + \frac{7}{12} + 1\frac{5}{8}$

_____   _____   _____

On Your Own

5 Marcel buys fabric to decorate a set for a school play. He buys $2\frac{2}{3}$ yards of green, $3\frac{1}{6}$ yards of blue, and $5\frac{1}{2}$ yards of black. How much fabric does Marcel buy?

_____

6 **Open Ended** Alex writes the expression $\frac{3}{11} + \frac{4}{5} + \frac{6}{11}$ on the board. Explain how you can use the properties of addition to find the sum.

_____

_____

_____

_____

7 **(MP) Model with Mathematics** The diagram shows the dimensions of a triangular flower bed. Write an addition expression to model the situation. What is the perimeter of the flower bed?

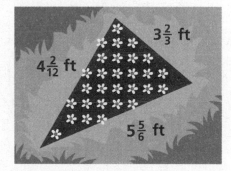

_____

Use the properties of addition to find the sum.

8 $\frac{1}{7} + (\frac{2}{7} + \frac{2}{3})$

9 $(\frac{1}{6} + \frac{2}{15}) + \frac{11}{15}$

_____

_____

10 $\frac{5}{12} + \frac{1}{3} + \frac{5}{12}$

11 $(1\frac{4}{5} + 2\frac{3}{4}) + 1\frac{3}{4}$

_____

_____

12 $3\frac{1}{6} + 5\frac{4}{9} + 2\frac{1}{6}$

13 $1\frac{4}{5} + (3\frac{2}{5} + 2\frac{1}{8})$

_____

_____

Use the properties of addition to find the sum.

14 $\left(\frac{5}{8} + 4\frac{2}{3}\right) + 1\frac{1}{8}$ **15** $4\frac{5}{18} + \frac{3}{4} + \frac{5}{18}$ **16** $\frac{7}{10} + 2\frac{4}{15} + 1\frac{1}{10}$

_____ _____ _____

17 (MP) **Use Structure** Valerie writes the expression $\left(\frac{1}{12} + \frac{4}{5}\right) + \left(\frac{1}{5} + \frac{7}{12}\right)$. How can she use the properties of addition to rewrite the expression so that it is easier to add?

_____

_____

18 The table shows the portion of three different types of pizzas that Nimal and Peter eat at a team party. All of the pizzas are the same size.

	Cheese	Veggie	Mushroom
Nimal	$\frac{1}{8}$	$\frac{3}{8}$	$\frac{1}{6}$
Peter	$\frac{1}{4}$	$\frac{1}{4}$	$\frac{1}{12}$

- Who eats more pizza, Nimal or Peter?

_____

- How much more pizza does this boy eat than the other?

_____

19 (MP) **Reason** Find the sum $\left(2\frac{1}{9} + 3\frac{3}{4}\right) + 3\frac{7}{9}$ without using the properties of addition. Would it have been easier to first use the properties of addition to reorder and regroup the addends? Explain your reasoning.

_____

_____

_____

Practice Addition and Subtraction Using Equations

(I Can) solve an addition or subtraction word problem by using an equation to model the problem.

Step It Out

1 After a run, Jared drinks $1\frac{3}{4}$ cups of water. His sister Emily drinks $1\frac{1}{2}$ cups more than Jared. How much water does Emily drink?

$1\frac{3}{4}$ c

Amount of Water Jared Drinks

A. Draw bar models to represent the problem.

Amount Jared drinks

Amount Emily drinks

?

Amount of Water Emily Drinks

B. Write an equation to model how much water Emily drinks.

_____

C. Estimate the answer. _____

D. Rename the mixed numbers with equivalent fractions using a common denominator. Then solve.

_____

E. How much water does Emily drink?

_____

F. Is your answer reasonable? Explain.

_____

 Turn and Talk Why is it a good idea to estimate the answer to a math problem?

Step It Out

2 After school, Sandra walks to the library. Then she walks home. What is the distance from the school to the library?

A. Write an addition equation and a related subtraction equation to model the problem. Use d for the distance from the school to the library.

_____

B. Estimate the answer. _____

C. Rename the mixed numbers as equivalent fractions with a common denominator. Then find the distance from the school to the library. Explain the process you use.

_____

_____

_____

D. Is your answer reasonable? Explain.

_____

Check Understanding Math Board

1 The Bakers spend $4\frac{1}{2}$ hours at the beach. They spend $2\frac{3}{5}$ hours in the water, and the rest of the time on land. Write an addition equation and a related subtraction equation to find t, the amount of time they spend on land. How much time do the Bakers spend on land?

_____

2 Lexi takes photos of food for magazine ads. At a photo shoot, she spends $\frac{5}{6}$ hour arranging the food and $1\frac{3}{4}$ hours taking photos of the food. Write an equation to model the number of hours Lexi spends at the photo shoot. How many hours is she at the photo shoot?

_____

On Your Own

3 (MP) **Model with Mathematics** Jason makes a kite that is $3\frac{7}{12}$ feet tall. Anne makes a kite that is $1\frac{1}{4}$ feet taller than Jason's kite. Draw a model to represent the problem and write an equation. How tall is Anne's kite?

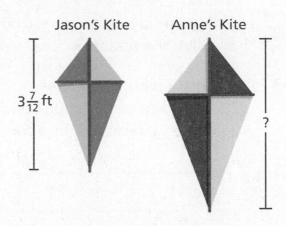

Jason's Kite   Anne's Kite

$3\frac{7}{12}$ ft

?

_____

_____

4 (MP) **Use Structure** David has $3\frac{1}{4}$ cups of flour. He needs $\frac{2}{3}$ cup to make biscuits and another $2\frac{3}{4}$ cups to make baguettes. Does David have enough flour? How much flour does David need or have left? Explain.

_____

_____

_____

_____

5 Mr. Lee's house has two stories and an attic. The first floor is $9\frac{1}{2}$ feet high, the second floor is $8\frac{3}{4}$ feet high, and the entire house is $24\frac{7}{12}$ feet high. What is the height of the attic?

_____

(MP) Model with Mathematics For 6 and 7, write an addition equation and a related subtraction equation to model the problem. Then solve the problem.

6 Roberta works on a science project for $6\frac{1}{6}$ hours. Her friend Jocelyn works on the project for $2\frac{2}{4}$ hours longer than Roberta. How long does Jocelyn work on the science project?

_____

_____

7 A cricket jumps away from a frog. Then it takes a second jump. How many inches is the cricket's first jump?

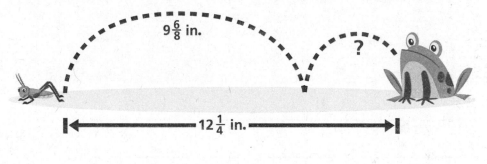

$9\frac{6}{8}$ in.

?

$12\frac{1}{4}$ in.

_____

_____

8 **(MP) Reason** Lauren measures $2\frac{1}{4}$ cups of flour for a recipe. She then realizes she needs to add $\frac{2}{3}$ cup of flour. Does Lauren use more than or less than 3 cups of flour? Explain.

_____

_____

9 **(MP) Model with Mathematics** A piece of quartz has a mass that is $2\frac{1}{2}$ kilograms greater than the mass of the granite. Write an equation to model the mass of the quartz. What is the mass of the quartz?

$6\frac{4}{5}$ kg

_____

_____

Review

Vocabulary

Complete each sentence by choosing a term from the Vocabulary Box.

1 You can use a _____ to compare and estimate fractions.

2 An _____ uses a different numerator and denominator to name the same part of a whole.

3 The _____ of two fractions is a common multiple of their denominators.

4 $\frac{1}{3} + \frac{3}{4} = \frac{3}{4} + \frac{1}{3}$ is an example of the

_____.

5 $(\frac{3}{8} + \frac{1}{6}) + \frac{5}{6} = \frac{3}{8} + (\frac{1}{6} + \frac{5}{6})$ is an example of the

_____.

Concepts and Skills

Estimate the sum or difference.

6 $\frac{4}{10} + \frac{7}{12}$ _____

7 $\frac{7}{8} - \frac{2}{5}$ _____

8 $14\frac{1}{3} - 3\frac{3}{4}$ _____

9 $5\frac{2}{12} + 6\frac{2}{3}$ _____

10 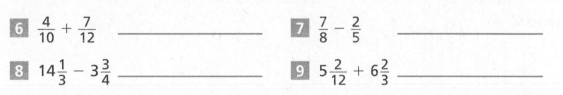 **Use Tools** Find $\frac{2}{3} + \frac{5}{6}$. Name the strategy or tool you will use to solve the problem, explain your choice, and then find the answer.

_____

_____

11 Which is equivalent to $\frac{10}{12} - \frac{1}{4}$?

(A) $\frac{9}{12}$ (B) $\frac{7}{12}$ (C) $\frac{1}{2}$ (D) $\frac{1}{3}$

12 The distance from Malik's home to a grocery store is 6 miles. The distance from his home to a park is $3\frac{3}{5}$ miles. How much farther from Malik's home is the grocery store than the park?

_____

13 Luisa writes a history report that is $2\frac{3}{4}$ pages long. Therese writes a report that is $1\frac{1}{2}$ pages longer than Luisa's report. How long is Therese's report?

_____

14 A bag of sunflower seeds weighs $5\frac{1}{2}$ pounds. Mr. Clark puts $1\frac{11}{16}$ pounds of the seeds in his bird feeder. How many pounds of sunflower seeds are left in the bag?

_____

15 Which is equivalent to the sum?

$2\frac{3}{4} + 1\frac{1}{3} + 2\frac{1}{4}$

(A) $6\frac{4}{12}$ (B) 6   (C) $5\frac{5}{11}$ (D) $5\frac{1}{3}$

16 Jessica works on her math homework. Then she works $1\frac{1}{5}$ hours on her science homework. She works a total of $4\frac{1}{4}$ hours on homework. Select all equations that Jessica could use to find m, the number of hours she works on her math homework.

(A) $m - 4\frac{1}{4} = 1\frac{1}{5}$

(B) $1\frac{1}{5} + 4\frac{1}{4} = m$

(C) $m + 1\frac{1}{5} = 4\frac{1}{4}$

(D) $m - 1\frac{1}{5} = 4\frac{1}{4}$

(E) $4\frac{1}{4} - 1\frac{1}{5} = m$

Multiply Fractions and Mixed Numbers

Chef

A chef does much more than cook food. A head chef is in charge of the kitchen, plans the menu, and sometimes writes the recipes. Chefs adjust the menu items in response to customers' needs such as special dietary restrictions or food allergies. Many chefs go to culinary school and work in an apprenticeship to get their start.

Did you know that there are other chefs in the kitchen? Other chefs are *sous chefs* (second in command), *chefs de partie* (station heads), and *commis* (beginner chefs).

Here's an interesting fact about food: When researchers in the UK and China teamed up to study the nutritional content of insects, they found that insects actually offered more nutrients than common protein sources.

STEM Task:

Find out what is meant by "processed food" and "good" carbohydrates. Then talk with your partner about what makes a healthful diet. Write down everything you eat or drink today. Then make a plan for how you might make more healthful choices tomorrow, such as choosing a salad instead of french fries for a side dish. Provide feedback for your partner's plan, and apply your partner's feedback to your plan.

Learning Mindset
Resilience Responds to Feedback

Sous chefs get guidance and feedback from the head chef. Athletes get guidance and feedback from the coach. Musicians get guidance and feedback from a master musician. Students get guidance and feedback from parents, guardians, teachers, and coaches. Guidance and feedback help you get better at whatever you are trying to learn. People who have your best interests in mind can give you helpful feedback. By listening to the feedback, you can make yourself better at the task at hand!

Reflect

Q Were you able to give and accept feedback effectively when speaking with a partner about a healthful diet?

Q What makes you receptive to feedback? What qualities does effective feedback have that less-effective feedback does not have?

Understand Multiplication of Fractions

How do **you** run a relay race?

- A track team enters a $\frac{6}{12}$-mile relay race. Any number of up to 6 runners can be on the team. However, if a team has more than one runner, then each runner must race an equal distance.

- Complete the table for 4 different numbers of runners. Write equations to show that each runner's distance multiplied by the number of runners equals the total distance of the race.

Number of Runners	Each Runner's Distance (miles)	Equation
1		
2		
3		
6		

 Turn and Talk

- How did you solve the problem?

- Which number of runners would you recommend that the track team use? Explain your reasoning.

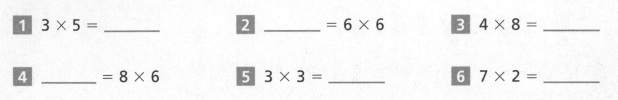
Are You Ready?

Complete these problems to review prior concepts and skills
you will need for this module.

Multiplication Facts

Find the product.

1 $3 \times 5 =$ _____

2 _____ $= 6 \times 6$

3 $4 \times 8 =$ _____

4 _____ $= 8 \times 6$

5 $3 \times 3 =$ _____

6 $7 \times 2 =$ _____

Multiply a Fraction by a Whole Number

Find the product.

7 $5 \times \frac{1}{8} =$ _____

8 $2 \times \frac{3}{7} =$ _____

9 $4 \times \frac{2}{5} =$ _____

10 $3 \times \frac{4}{12} =$ _____

11 $5 \times \frac{2}{15} =$ _____

12 $7 \times \frac{1}{3} =$ _____

Rename Fractions and Mixed Numbers

Write the mixed number as a fraction.

13 $1\frac{1}{2} =$ _____

14 $2\frac{1}{4} =$ _____

15 $2\frac{3}{10} =$ _____

16 $4\frac{2}{3} =$ _____

Write the fraction as a mixed number.

17 $\frac{9}{8} =$ _____

18 $\frac{7}{3} =$ _____

19 $\frac{11}{5} =$ _____

20 $\frac{14}{5} =$ _____

Name

Explore Groups of Equal Shares to Show Multiplication

(I Can) find a fractional part of a group by using a visual model to solve a problem.

Spark Your Learning

Ayesha writes a children's story about quartets of cat musicians. In her story, $\frac{1}{4}$ of the cats in two quartets play the cello. How many cats in two quartets play the cello?

Draw a visual model to show how you can find the number of cats in two quartets that play the cello. Justify your reasoning.

SMALL GROUPS

Turn and Talk How could you find the number of cats that do not play the cello?

Build Understanding

1 After their concert, the cat quartet invites their friends to a party. Of the total number of cats shown, $\frac{1}{6}$ of the cats have striped tails. How many cats have striped tails?

Draw a visual model to show how you can find the number of cats that have striped tails.

A. How is the **unit fraction** $\frac{1}{6}$ represented in your visual model?

_____

_____

_____

B. How can you use your visual model to find the number of cats that have striped tails?

_____

C. How many cats have striped tails? _____

Turn and Talk How would your visual model change if you wanted to find $\frac{1}{2}$ of the cats at the party instead of $\frac{1}{6}$?

2 Four more cats join the party. Of the cats shown, $\frac{3}{4}$ have solid-colored tails. How many cats have solid-colored tails?

Draw a visual model to show how you can find the number of cats that have solid-colored tails.

A. How many equal-sized groups did you draw? Why?

_____

B. How many cats are represented in each group? _____

C. How many of these groups represent cats with solid-colored tails? How do you know?

_____

D. How many cats have solid-colored tails? _____

Check Understanding [Math Board]

1 At nine o'clock, $\frac{5}{8}$ of the 16 cats at a party go home. How many cats go home at nine o'clock? Draw a visual model to find the answer.

_____

On Your Own

2 (MP) **Reason** Walt has twenty $1 bills. He uses $\frac{3}{5}$ of his $1 bills to pay for a new winter hat. How much does Walt pay for his new winter hat? How do you know?

_____

_____

3 (MP) **Use Repeated Reasoning** Seth buys a carton of eggs. Find the number of eggs in each fraction of the total.

- $\frac{2}{3}$ of the eggs _____
- $\frac{5}{6}$ of the eggs _____
- $\frac{1}{9}$ of the eggs _____
- $\frac{6}{9}$ of the eggs _____

Draw a visual model to solve.

4 $\frac{2}{5}$ of 15 _____

5 $\frac{5}{6}$ of 12 _____

6 (MP) **Use Tools** Use the number line to find $\frac{7}{8}$ of 24. _____

```
<----|----|----|----|----|----|----|----|---->
     0                             24
```

I'm in a Learning Mindset!

What strategies did I use to show a fractional part of a group?

_____

Represent Multiplication of Whole Numbers by Fractions

(I Can) find the product of a whole number and a fraction using a visual model.

Spark Your Learning

Earl bakes 3 loaves of bread. He keeps $\frac{1}{4}$ of the bread for himself and gives the rest to his neighbors. How many loaves of bread does Earl give to his neighbors?

Draw a visual model to show how you can find how many loaves he gives away. Justify your reasoning.

SMALL GROUPS

Turn and Talk How would your visual model change if Earl decides to keep $\frac{1}{8}$ of the bread instead of $\frac{1}{4}$?

Build Understanding

1 Mrs. Fan bakes 2 cakes, each in the shape of a hexagon. She takes $\frac{3}{4}$ of the cakes to a party.

Determine how much cake she takes to the party using pattern blocks and then draw a visual model to show your work.

A. How did you use pattern blocks to find the amount of cake Mrs. Fan takes to the party?

_____

_____

_____

B. What amount of the two cakes does Mrs. Fan take to the party?

_____

C. Write a multiplication equation to model the problem.

_____

 Turn and Talk Why is it not appropriate to model this situation with the expression $2 \times \frac{3}{4}$?

2 Rashad bakes 4 equal-sized granola bars. He serves $\frac{2}{3}$ of the bars to his friends.

Draw a visual model to show how you can find how many granola bars he serves.

A. How did you make equal-sized parts from 4 wholes? What does each part represent?

_____

_____

B. What does the 2 in the fraction $\frac{2}{3}$ represent? How did you show this in your visual model?

_____

_____

C. How many $\frac{1}{3}$-size pieces does he serve? _____

D. How many granola bars does he serve? Write a multiplication equation to model the problem.

_____

 Turn and Talk How could you rearrange your visual model to find the number of whole bars Rashad serves? Explain.

3 Isa has 2 boxes of pizza. Each box has $\frac{5}{8}$ of a pizza left. Jack says that this story context can be modeled with the equation $\frac{5}{8} \times 2 = 1\frac{1}{4}$.

A. Explain why Jack's equation does not model the story context.

_____

_____

B. Rewrite the story context so that it can be modeled with the equation $\frac{5}{8} \times 2 = 1\frac{1}{4}$. Then draw a visual model to represent the problem.

_____

_____

Check Understanding 〔Math Board〕

1 Al bakes 4 round cakes that are decorated like baseballs for a team party. The party guests eat $\frac{7}{8}$ of the cakes. How many cakes do they eat in all? Draw a visual model to find the answer. Then write an equation to model the problem.

_____

2 A carpenter has 10 equal-sized pieces of wood. She uses $\frac{3}{5}$ of the wood to make a box. Use a visual model to find the number of pieces of wood that the carpenter uses. Then write an equation to model the problem.

_____

On Your Own

3 (MP) **Use Structure** Megan makes four giant oatmeal cookies and cuts them into equal-sized pieces. She puts $\frac{11}{12}$ of the cookies into a cookie jar. In a visual model for this situation:

- How many wholes do you need? _____

- What is the fewest number of equal-sized pieces you should cut each cookie into if you want to put $\frac{11}{12}$ of the cookies in the jar?

  _____

- How many cookies go into the jar?

  _____

Draw a visual model to find the product.

4 $\frac{3}{8} \times 4 =$

_____

5 $\frac{2}{9} \times 3 =$

_____

6 (MP) **Attend to Precision** How could you use a visual model to show the product $\frac{14}{15} \times 3$? Explain.

_____

_____

_____

7 **Open Ended** Write a story problem for the given equation.

$$\frac{2}{3} \times 12 = 8$$

_____

_____

_____

8 (MP) **Use Tools** Use the number line to find $\frac{7}{8}$ of 16.

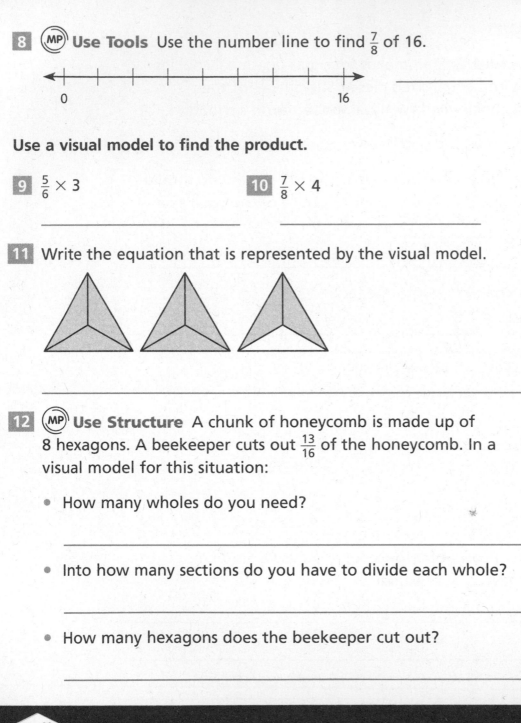

0   16   _____

Use a visual model to find the product.

9 $\frac{5}{6} \times 3$

10 $\frac{7}{8} \times 4$

_____   _____

11 Write the equation that is represented by the visual model.

_____

12 (MP) **Use Structure** A chunk of honeycomb is made up of 8 hexagons. A beekeeper cuts out $\frac{13}{16}$ of the honeycomb. In a visual model for this situation:

• How many wholes do you need?

_____

• Into how many sections do you have to divide each whole?

_____

• How many hexagons does the beekeeper cut out?

_____

🔷 I'm in a Learning Mindset!

What type of feedback can I provide about strategies for multiplying whole numbers by fractions?

_____

_____

Name

Represent Multiplication with Unit Fractions

(I Can) solve a problem by multiplying unit fractions using a visual model.

Spark Your Learning

A chef uses $\frac{1}{4}$ of a package of dough. Before using this part of the package of dough, she cuts it into thirds. What fraction of a whole package is each of these smaller pieces?

Draw a visual model to show the problem. Justify how your visual model represents the problem.

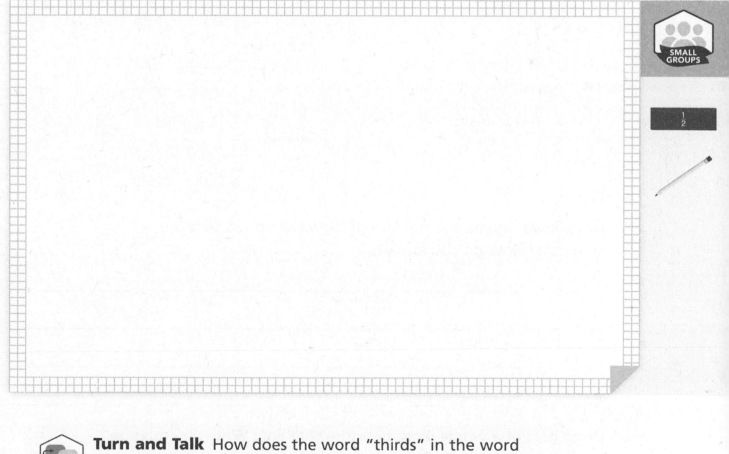

Turn and Talk How does the word "thirds" in the word problem help you set up your visual model?

Build Understanding

1 Only $\frac{1}{3}$ of a chef's specialty pizza is left at closing time. The chef eats $\frac{1}{2}$ of the leftover pizza. How much of the whole pizza does the chef eat?

Draw a visual model to show the fraction of the whole pizza that the chef eats. Justify your reasoning.

A. How do you name the fraction of the whole pizza that the chef eats? How do you know?

_____

_____

_____

_____

B. What part of a whole pizza does the chef eat? Write an equation to model the problem.

_____

2 The chef also makes stromboli. One serving is $\frac{1}{2}$ of a stromboli. What fraction of a meter is the length of one serving?

Use the number line to show how you can find the length of one serving.

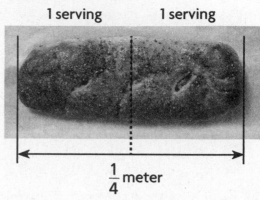

1 serving   1 serving

$\frac{1}{4}$ meter

0 ——————————————— 1

A. What fraction of a meter is one serving of stromboli? How do you know?

_____

_____

_____

B. Write an equation to model the problem. _____

 Turn and Talk How would your number line change if the stromboli were cut into thirds instead of halves?

· ·

Check Understanding [Math Board]

1 The chef makes a rectangular pizza. At closing time, $\frac{1}{6}$ of the pizza is left. The chef eats $\frac{1}{2}$ of the leftover pizza. Draw a visual model to find the fraction of a whole pizza that the chef eats.

Write an equation to model the problem.

_____

2 Use the number line to show $\frac{1}{5} \times \frac{1}{2}$.

0 ——————————————— 1

On Your Own

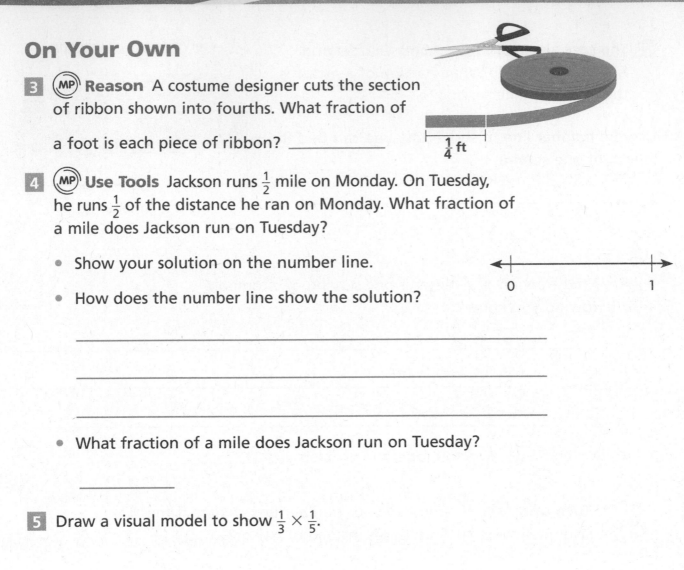

3 (MP) **Reason** A costume designer cuts the section of ribbon shown into fourths. What fraction of

a foot is each piece of ribbon? _____

$\frac{1}{4}$ ft

4 (MP) **Use Tools** Jackson runs $\frac{1}{2}$ mile on Monday. On Tuesday, he runs $\frac{1}{2}$ of the distance he ran on Monday. What fraction of a mile does Jackson run on Tuesday?

• Show your solution on the number line.

• How does the number line show the solution?

0   1

_____

_____

_____

• What fraction of a mile does Jackson run on Tuesday?

_____

5 Draw a visual model to show $\frac{1}{3} \times \frac{1}{5}$.

🔢 I'm in a Learning Mindset!

How would I describe my understanding of using visual models to represent the product of two unit fractions? What can I tell myself to stay positive about my progress?

_____

_____

Name

Represent Multiplication of Fractions

(I Can) multiply fractions using a visual model.

Spark Your Learning

Alejandro and Prisha are practicing their soccer skills. Alejandro kicks his soccer ball $\frac{4}{5}$ of the length of the field. Prisha kicks her ball $\frac{3}{4}$ of the distance Alejandro kicks his ball. How far down the soccer field does Prisha kick her ball?

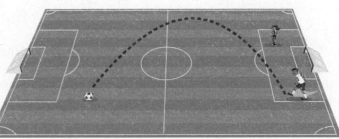

Draw a visual model to show how far down the soccer field Prisha kicks her ball.

SMALL GROUPS

 Turn and Talk How could you determine that Prisha kicked the ball a lesser distance than Alejandro without solving the problem?

Build Understanding

1 Prisha has been practicing her kicking skills so that she can beat Alejandro. During another practice she kicks her soccer ball $\frac{5}{6}$ of the length of the field. Alejandro kicks his soccer ball $\frac{4}{5}$ of the distance Prisha kicks her ball.

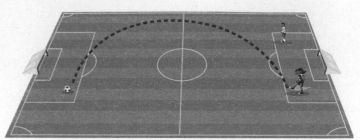

Use the number line to show how far down the soccer field Alejandro kicks his ball.

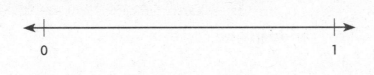

0   1

A. What does the 1 on the number line represent?

_____

B. How did you represent Prisha's distance?

_____

_____

C. How did you represent Alejandro's distance?

_____

_____

_____

D. How far down the field does Alejandro kick his soccer ball? Write an equation to model the problem.

_____

2 After soccer, Prisha and Alejandro are hungry. Prisha eats $\frac{6}{8}$ of a granola bar. Alejandro eats $\frac{2}{3}$ as much as Prisha eats.

Draw a visual model to show the fraction of a whole granola bar that Alejandro eats.

A. How much of a whole granola bar does Alejandro eat? How does your visual model show this?

_____

_____

_____

B. Write an equation to model the problem.

_____

Check Understanding · Math Board

1 Jake's family eats $\frac{3}{8}$ of a pan of banana bread. Emily's family eats $\frac{2}{3}$ of the amount that Jake's family eats. How much of a whole pan of banana bread does Emily's family eat? Write an equation to model the problem.

_____

On Your Own

2 (MP) **Reason** A recipe for honey-glazed chicken calls for $\frac{3}{4}$ cup of honey. Marcel wants to make $\frac{2}{3}$ of a batch of the recipe. Use the number line to find the amount of honey that he needs. Write an equation to model the problem.

_____

3 (MP) **Model with Mathematics** Write a story problem that can be modeled with the equation $\frac{1}{4} \times \frac{8}{12} = \frac{2}{12}$. Then draw a visual model to represent the problem.

_____

_____

_____

Draw a visual model to solve.

4 $\frac{5}{6} \times \frac{6}{7} =$ _____

5 $\frac{2}{3} \times \frac{9}{10} =$ _____

⬡ I'm in a Learning Mindset!

How did the feedback I provided for making visual models affect others in my class?

_____

Name _____

Use Representations of Area to Develop Procedures

(I Can) find the product of fractions using an area model.

Spark Your Learning

A contractor buys rectangular floor tiles for a home that he is building. How can you find the area of the tile?

Use the square to help you find the area of the tile. Explain your reasoning.

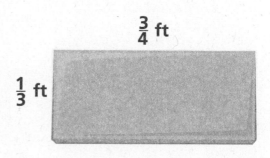

$\frac{3}{4}$ ft

$\frac{1}{3}$ ft

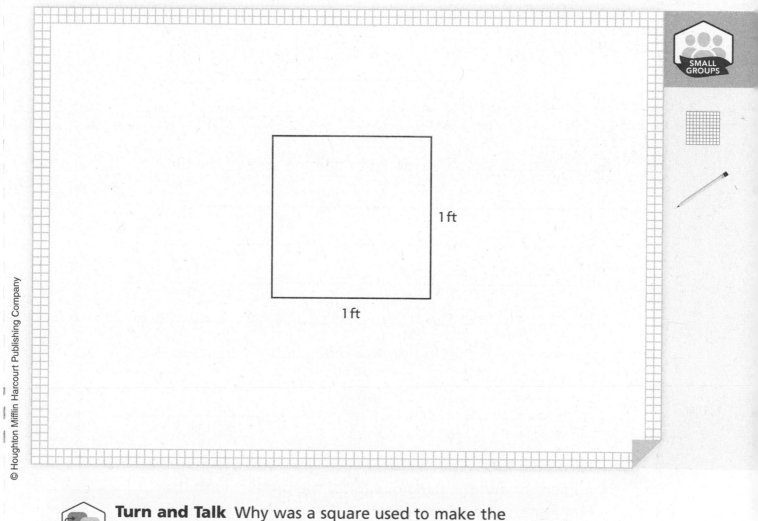

1 ft

1 ft

SMALL GROUPS

Turn and Talk Why was a square used to make the visual model?

Build Understanding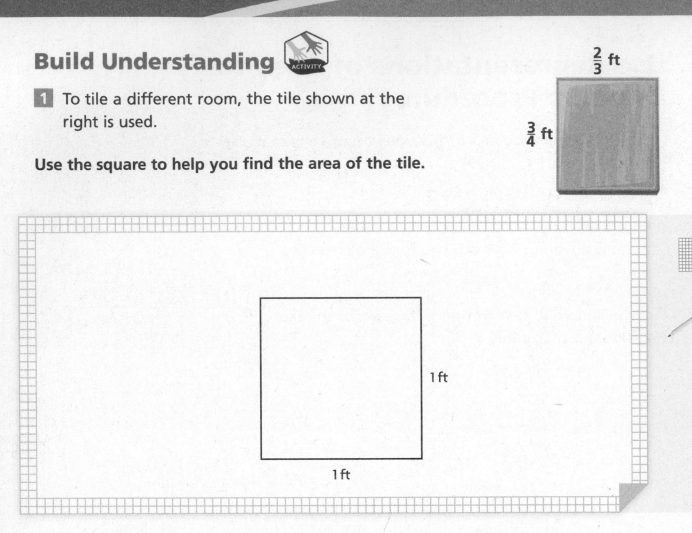

1 To tile a different room, the tile shown at the right is used.

Use the square to help you find the area of the tile.

$\frac{2}{3}$ ft

$\frac{3}{4}$ ft

1 ft

1 ft

A. How can you use your area model to find the area of the tile?

_____

_____

_____

_____

B. What is the area of the tile? Write a multiplication equation to model the problem.

_____

 Turn and Talk What do you notice when you compare the numerator and the denominator of the product with the numerators and denominators in the factors?

Name _____

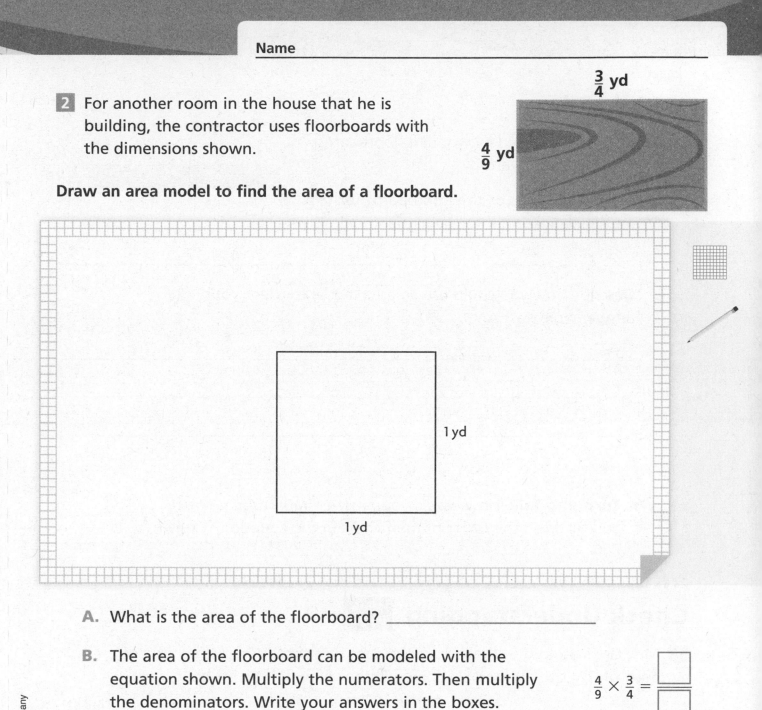

2 For another room in the house that he is building, the contractor uses floorboards with the dimensions shown.

$\frac{3}{4}$ yd

$\frac{4}{9}$ yd

Draw an area model to find the area of a floorboard.

1 yd

1 yd

A. What is the area of the floorboard? _____

B. The area of the floorboard can be modeled with the equation shown. Multiply the numerators. Then multiply the denominators. Write your answers in the boxes.

$\frac{4}{9} \times \frac{3}{4} = \dfrac{\boxed{}}{\boxed{}}$

C. Compare your answers from Parts A and B.

_____

D. How can you find the product of two fractions without using a visual model? Explain your thinking.

_____

_____

_____

Step It Out

3 A store is selling new wooden floorboards that measure $\frac{2}{3}$ yard by $\frac{1}{12}$ yard.

$\frac{2}{3}$ yd

$\frac{1}{12}$ yd

A. What is the area of the floorboard? Write a multiplication equation to model the problem.

_____

B. Describe how you could use an area model to check your answer from Part A.

_____

_____

_____

 Turn and Talk How would your answer in Part A change if you reversed the order of the factors in the equation? Explain.

Check Understanding `Math Board`

1 Mrs. Lin is using tiles that measure $\frac{1}{2}$ foot by $\frac{2}{3}$ foot. What is the area of each tile? Write a multiplication equation to model the problem.

_____

2 To fit in a corner, a contractor cuts the tile shown in half. What is the area of one piece of the cut tile? Write a multiplication equation to model the area.

$\frac{1}{3}$ ft

$\frac{5}{6}$ ft

_____

Find the product.

3 $\frac{3}{8} \times \frac{2}{3}$

4 $\frac{4}{9} \times \frac{3}{5}$

5 $\frac{3}{2} \times \frac{9}{12}$

On Your Own

6 (MP) **Attend to Precision** A farm field measures $\frac{3}{8}$ mile wide by $\frac{2}{3}$ mile long. What fraction of a square mile is the area of the field? Explain how you found your answer.

_____

_____

7 (MP) **Use Tools** Mr. Chiu has a large box for wet boots in his classroom. He wants to put plastic sheeting under the box. The dimensions of the bottom are $\frac{3}{4}$ yard and $\frac{7}{8}$ yard. How much sheeting does he need?

• Use the square to find the area of the bottom of the box.

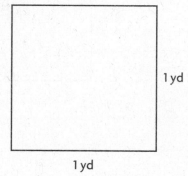

1 yd

1 yd

• How many small rectangles represent the area of the bottom of the box? What area does each small rectangle drawn in your model represent?

_____

• How much sheeting does he need? Write an equation to model the problem.

_____

Find the product.

8 $\frac{5}{6} \times \frac{2}{5}$

9 $\frac{3}{8} \times \frac{3}{7}$

10 $\frac{3}{5} \times \frac{5}{8}$

_____   _____   _____

11 (MP) **Use Structure** Explain how you can find the product $\frac{1}{2} \times \frac{2}{3} \times \frac{3}{4}$ using area models.

_____

_____

_____

_____

_____

12 (MP) **Use Tools** Use the square to find the area of the rectangle shown.

$\frac{5}{8}$ ft

$\frac{3}{4}$ ft

1 ft

1 ft

Area = _____

13 A sheet of paper measures $\frac{7}{12}$ foot by $\frac{7}{8}$ foot. What is the area of the sheet of paper?

_____

➗ I'm in a Learning Mindset!

How did I use feedback my teacher gave me?

_____

_____

Name _____

Interpret Fraction Multiplication as Scaling

(I Can) explain how the size of the product compares to the size of one factor.

Spark Your Learning

The painting shown is resized to $\frac{3}{4}$ of its original size. How does the height of the resized painting compare to the height of the original painting? Is the height of the resized painting more than or less than $\frac{3}{4}$ foot?

Draw a visual model to represent your thinking. Justify your reasoning.

$\frac{3}{4}$ ft

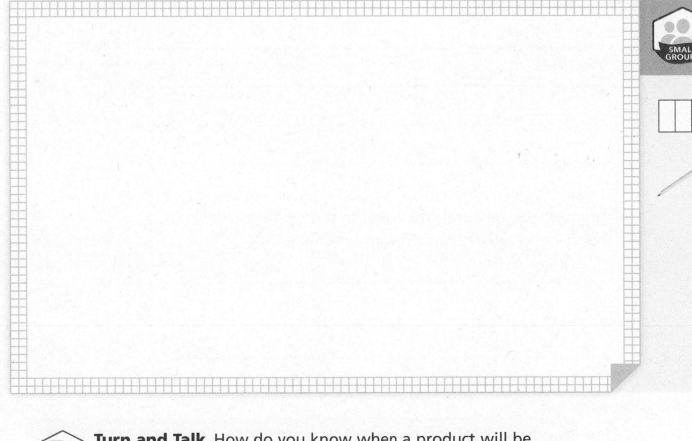

SMALL GROUPS

 Turn and Talk How do you know when a product will be less than one of its factors?

Build Understanding

1. A roller hockey puck typically weighs $\frac{1}{4}$ pound. An ice hockey puck typically weighs $\frac{3}{2}$ times as much as a roller hockey puck.

   A. Write a multiplication expression to model the problem. _____

   B. How do your factors from Part A compare to 1?

   _____

   C. What is the product of a number multiplied by 1?

   _____

   D. Will the product of a number multiplied by a factor greater than 1 be less than or greater than that number? How do you know?

   _____

   _____

   _____

   _____

   E. Predict whether the typical weight of an ice hockey puck is greater than, less than, or equal to the typical weight of a roller hockey puck. Explain your reasoning.

   _____

   _____

   _____

   _____

   Turn and Talk By what fractions could you multiply $\frac{1}{4}$ to get a product that is less than $\frac{1}{4}$? Equal to $\frac{1}{4}$? Explain.

Step It Out

2 A new skateboard ramp is designed that has a width that is $\frac{2}{3}$ of the width of the ramp shown.

$\frac{5}{6}$ yd

A. Is the width of the new ramp greater than or less than the width of the ramp shown? How do you know?

_____

_____

_____

B. By what factor could the new ramp be resized so that the width is greater than the width of the original ramp? Explain.

_____

Turn and Talk What would the scale factor have to be if you wanted the width of the ramp to stay the same? Explain.

Check Understanding 〔Math Board〕

1 A vehicle traveling 70 miles each hour needs $\frac{1}{10}$ mile to come to a complete stop. Engineers are designing a new vehicle that can come to a complete stop in $\frac{1}{2}$ of that distance. How does the stopping distance of the new vehicle compare to the stopping distance of the original vehicle?

_____

A $\frac{3}{8}$-yard-long toy bus is rescaled as modeled by the expressions shown in 2–4. Use *shorter*, *longer*, or *same* to describe how the length of the rescaled bus compares to the original length.

2 $\frac{8}{1} \times \frac{3}{8}$ **3** $\frac{8}{8} \times \frac{3}{8}$ **4** $\frac{1}{2} \times \frac{3}{8}$

_____   _____   _____

On Your Own

5 **STEM** Human and animal brains are made of millions of neurons. Dogs have about 530,000,000 brain neurons. Cats have about $\frac{1}{2}$ of this amount of brain neurons. Which animal has more brain neurons? Explain.

_____

For 6–8, complete the statement with _equal to_, _greater than_, or _less than_.

6 $\frac{4}{5} \times \frac{1}{3}$ will be _____ $\frac{1}{3}$.

7 $1 \times \frac{1}{4}$ will be _____ $\frac{1}{4}$.

8 $6 \times \frac{2}{5}$ will be _____ $\frac{2}{5}$.

Chicago's Willis Tower measures 1,729 feet tall at its tip. The tower is rescaled as modeled by the expressions shown in 9–11. Use _shorter_, _taller_, or _same_ to describe how the height of the rescaled tower compares to the original height.

9 $\frac{9}{9} \times 1,729$ **10** $\frac{2}{1} \times 1,729$ **11** $\frac{1}{9} \times 1,729$

_____   _____   _____

12 **(MP)** **Construct Arguments** Carl and Maeve are asked to think of a fraction and multiply it by 5,267. Carl thinks of $\frac{5}{6}$. Maeve thinks of $\frac{7}{7}$. They both say their product is less than 5,267. Are they correct? Explain.

_____

_____

✦ I'm in a Learning Mindset!

What helps me go from one learning activity to a different one?

_____

Name _____

Multiply Fractions

(I Can) solve problems involving the multiplication of a whole
number or fraction by a fraction.

Step It Out

1 An annual fundraiser raised $\frac{4}{5}$ of the
amount of money in 2017 as it did in
2018. Five-thousand dollars was raised
in 2018. How much money was raised
in 2017?

A. In which year do you think more money
was raised? Explain your reasoning.

_____

_____

_____

_____

B. Write an equation to model the problem. Write the whole
number factor as a fraction.

_____

C. Solve the equation $4 \times 5{,}000 \div 5 = r$. How does this
equation compare to your equation from Part B?

_____

_____

D. How much money was raised in 2017? Write your answer as
a whole number. How does your answer compare to your
answer from Part A?

_____

_____

2 A soccer team is having a fundraiser. Of the items they are selling, $\frac{3}{4}$ are gift cards. Two-thirds of the gift cards are restaurant gift cards.

A. What fraction of the items they are selling are restaurant gift cards? Write an equation to model the problem.

_____

B. Describe how you could have used a visual model to find the answer.

_____

_____

_____

_____

_____

 Turn and Talk How do you know your answer is reasonable?

Check Understanding [Math Board]

1 Of the movies in Mr. Jackson's collection, $\frac{7}{10}$ are on DVD. Of those, $\frac{1}{2}$ are science fiction movies. What fraction of Mr. Jackson's movies are science fiction DVDs?

_____

Find the product.

2 $\frac{3}{8} \times 16$

3 $\frac{1}{2} \times \frac{3}{5}$

4 $\frac{1}{3} \times 4$

_____ _____ _____

On Your Own

5 (MP) **Use Structure** Does the order of the factors change the product? Explain.

$18 \times \frac{3}{8} =$ ▩ $\frac{3}{8} \times 18 =$ ▩

_____

_____

Find the product.

6 $\frac{5}{9} \times 18$ 7 $32 \times \frac{2}{3}$ 8 $\frac{7}{8} \times \frac{9}{10}$

_____   _____   _____

9 Evaluate the numerical expression. $\frac{5}{6} \times (16 - 4)$

  • Which operation do you perform first? _____

  • Write this answer as a fraction. _____

  • What is the product of the numerators? _____

  • What is the product of the denominators? _____

  • What is the value of the numerical expression? _____

10 Explain how to find $\frac{11}{12}$ of 4 by evaluating the numerical expression $11 \times 4 \div 12$.

_____

_____

11 (MP) **Reason** Sam is using craft felt to carpet two rooms in a dollhouse. Both rooms are $\frac{5}{6}$ feet by $\frac{7}{8}$ feet. How many square feet of craft felt does Sam need to carpet both rooms? Explain your reasoning.

_____

_____

_____

12 (MP) **Model with Mathematics** The British Telecom Tower is about $\frac{3}{7}$ the height of the Empire State Building. Write two different numerical expressions to model the height of the British Telecom Tower.

_____

443 m

13 (MP) **Use Structure** Kasim picks 8 pounds of strawberries. He uses $\frac{5}{8}$ of the strawberries to make a fruit salad. Then he uses $\frac{2}{3}$ of the remaining strawberries to make fruit smoothies. How many pounds of strawberries does Kasim have left after

making fruit salad and smoothies? _____

Empire State Building

Find the product.

14 $\frac{3}{5} \times 7 =$ _____

15 $\frac{1}{8} \times \frac{2}{3} =$ _____

16 $\frac{9}{11} \times (5 \times 3) =$ _____

17 $\frac{17}{20} \times (12 \div 2) =$ _____

18 (MP) **Reason** Will the product be _greater than_, _less than_, or _equal to_ 34? Explain your reasoning.

$$\frac{1}{3} \times \frac{1}{3} \times \frac{1}{3} \times 34$$

_____

_____

19 (MP) **Construct Arguments** Jorge models the area of the rectangle with the equation $\frac{2}{3} \times 3 = m$. Caleb models the area of the rectangle with the equation $2 \times 3 \div 3 = p$. Which equation is correct? Explain your reasoning.

$\frac{2}{3}$ ft

3 ft

_____

_____

_____

_____

Name _____

Review

Concepts and Skills

1 (MP) **Use Tools** Of the 10 dancers at the international dance competition, $\frac{3}{5}$ of them are from Asia. How many dancers are from Asia? Tell what strategy or tool you will use to answer the question, explain your choice, and then find the answer.

_____

2 At the beach, Mae fills 6 buckets with sand. She uses $\frac{2}{3}$ of the sand in the buckets to make a sand castle. How many buckets of sand does Mae use to build the sand castle?

_____

3 How could you use a visual model to show $\frac{3}{10} \times 5$? Explain.

_____

_____

_____

4 Mr. Diaz is 50 years old. Ms. Lowe is $\frac{4}{5}$ as old as Mr. Diaz. Who is younger, Mr. Diaz or Ms. Lowe? Explain.

_____

5 Overnight, $\frac{1}{2}$ foot of snow fell. By noon the next day, $\frac{1}{4}$ of the fallen snow had melted. How much snow had melted? Use the number

line to find the answer. _____

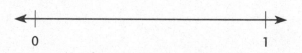

6 Draw an area model to find the area of a tile that measures $\frac{1}{4}$ inch by $\frac{1}{4}$ inch.

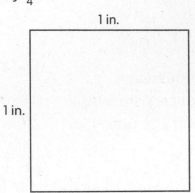

1 in.

1 in.

---

7 A speckled padloper turtle weighs $\frac{5}{16}$ pound. A pygmy mouse lemur weighs $\frac{2}{5}$ of the weight of the speckled padloper turtle. What is the weight of the pygmy mouse lemur?

Ⓐ $\frac{10}{80}$ pound

Ⓒ $\frac{3}{16}$ pound

Ⓑ $\frac{25}{32}$ pound

Ⓓ $\frac{1}{2}$ pound

8 Jamal is building a playhouse for cats. The first level measures $\frac{3}{4}$ yard by $\frac{1}{2}$ yard. The second level measures $\frac{2}{3}$ yard by $\frac{3}{8}$ yard. Jamal wants to carpet both levels. How many square yards of carpeting does he need?

---

9 Select all the expressions that have a value less than 9,721.

Ⓐ $\frac{3}{4} \times 9{,}721$

Ⓑ $\frac{4}{3} \times 9{,}721$

Ⓒ $\frac{2}{3} \times 9{,}721$

Ⓓ $1\frac{3}{4} \times 9{,}721$

Ⓔ $3 \times 9{,}721$

Ⓕ $\frac{3}{2} \times 9{,}721$

Understand and Apply Multiplication of Mixed Numbers

WHICH DOES NOT BELONG?

- Look at the figures below. Each figure is a circle that is missing a piece.

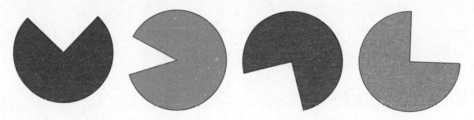

- Which figure is different from the others?

_____

What is different about it?

_____

_____

- Write an expression to model the total amount of the four figures.

_____

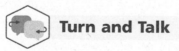 **Turn and Talk**

- How did you know the fraction of a whole circle represented by each figure?

- What other expression could you write for this problem?

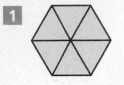
Are You Ready?

Complete these problems to review prior concepts and skills you will need for this module.

Fractions Equal to 1

Write the fraction that names the whole.

1  $\dfrac{\square}{\square}$ = 1 whole

2 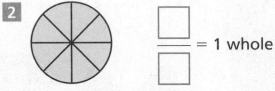 $\dfrac{\square}{\square}$ = 1 whole

Multiplication Facts

Find the product.

3 $6 \times 4 =$ _____

4 $7 \times 7 =$ _____

5 $9 \times 5 =$ _____

6 _____ $= 10 \times 8$

7 $2 \times 6 =$ _____

8 $7 \times 8 =$ _____

9 _____ $= 7 \times 9$

10 _____ $= 4 \times 4$

11 _____ $= 3 \times 8$

12 _____ $= 4 \times 3$

13 _____ $= 2 \times 9$

14 _____ $= 5 \times 5$

Rename Fractions and Mixed Numbers

Write the mixed number as a fraction.

15 $3\frac{1}{5} =$ _____

16 $4\frac{2}{5} =$ _____

17 $6\frac{3}{4} =$ _____

18 $3\frac{5}{8} =$ _____

Write the fraction as a mixed number.

19 $\frac{16}{3} =$ _____

20 $\frac{10}{7} =$ _____

21 $\frac{52}{9} =$ _____

22 $\frac{17}{3} =$ _____

Name _____

Explore Area and Mixed Numbers

(I Can) use an area model to multiply mixed numbers.

Spark Your Learning

Ms. Cruz wants to use square tiles to cover the front entryway of a house. Each tile she plans to use measures $\frac{1}{2}$ foot by $\frac{1}{2}$ foot. What is the area of the entryway?

Draw a visual model to show how many tiles she will use. Then explain how you can use your visual model to find the area of the entryway.

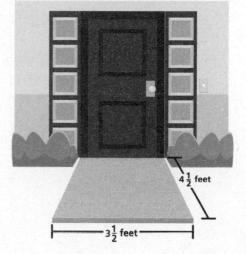

$4\frac{1}{2}$ feet

$3\frac{1}{2}$ feet

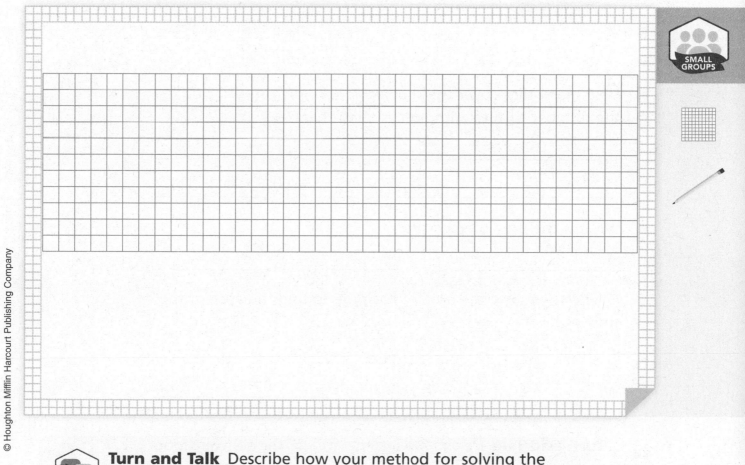

SMALL GROUPS

Turn and Talk Describe how your method for solving the problem would change if Ms. Cruz uses smaller tiles that each measure $\frac{1}{4}$ foot by $\frac{1}{4}$ foot.

Build Understanding

1. Will replaces the tiles of a shower floor. The floor measures $4\frac{1}{3}$ feet by $3\frac{2}{3}$ feet. Will covers the floor with small square tiles. Each tile he uses is $\frac{1}{3}$ foot by $\frac{1}{3}$ foot.

   Use the grid to represent the shower floor. Each square represents one tile.

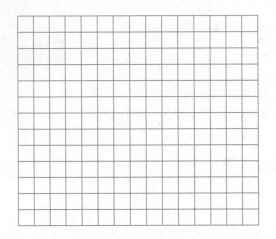

A. How many tiles cover the shower floor? How can you find the number of tiles without counting them?

_____

_____

B. What is the area of each tile?

_____

C. How can you use the area of each tile to find the area of the shower floor?

_____

D. What is the area of the shower floor? _____

 Turn and Talk Donna models the area of the shower floor as $\frac{13}{3} \times \frac{11}{3}$. How is this like the method you used to find the area? How is it different?

2 What is the area of this map?

$2\frac{1}{2}$ feet

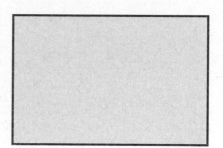

You can use an area model to multiply mixed numbers.

$1\frac{7}{8}$ feet

A. How can you rewrite each mixed number as the sum of a whole number and a fraction?

_____

B. Use the rectangle to draw an area model by drawing a vertical line and a horizontal line to show how you broke apart the mixed numbers in Part A. Label the side lengths of the four smaller rectangles.

C. What equations model the areas of the four smaller rectangles?

_____

D. How can you use the areas of the four rectangles to find the area of the map? What is the area of the map?

_____

• •

Check Understanding Math Board

1 Pat cuts fabric for the back panel of a jacket. He measures it to be $1\frac{2}{3}$ feet long and $1\frac{1}{3}$ feet wide. He represents the area on a grid. The side length of each small square in the grid represents $\frac{1}{3}$ foot. What is the area of the panel? Show your work.

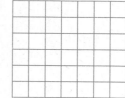

_____

Use the rectangle to draw an area model to solve.

2 $2\frac{1}{3} \times 3\frac{1}{2}$

_____

On Your Own

3 Use the grid to find $1\frac{1}{4} \times 3\frac{1}{4}$. Let each square represent $\frac{1}{4}$ foot by $\frac{1}{4}$ foot.

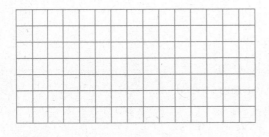

4 Use the rectangle to draw an area model to find $2\frac{1}{2} \times 4\frac{2}{3}$.

_____

_____

5 **Open Ended** Chris is building a rectangular-shaped patio using square tiles. Each tile has a side length of $\frac{1}{6}$ yard. The patio should be between 2 yards and 3 yards long and between 1 yard and 2 yards wide. Choose a length and a width for the patio. What is the area of the patio? Explain your method.

_____

_____

_____

_____

I'm in a Learning Mindset!

What strategies did I use to multiply mixed numbers?

_____

_____

Name

Multiply Mixed Numbers

(I Can) solve real world problems involving multiplication of mixed numbers by writing an equation to model the problem.

Spark Your Learning

Arun paints on a large rectangular canvas that measures $2\frac{1}{4}$ feet by $4\frac{1}{3}$ feet. He wants to enter his painting into an art contest. The contest rules say that the area of all canvases must be less than $4\frac{1}{3}$ square feet.

Based on these rules, can Arun enter his painting into the contest? Explain with words or drawings.

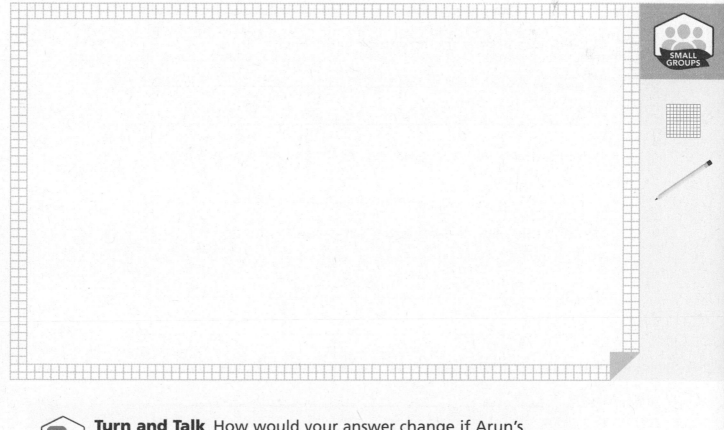

Turn and Talk How would your answer change if Arun's canvas measured $\frac{5}{6}$ foot by $4\frac{1}{3}$ feet? Justify your reasoning.

Build Understanding

1 Tam draws a logo for her company's website. The logo is a rectangle that is $1\frac{1}{3}$ inches wide and $1\frac{3}{4}$ inches long. What is the area of the logo?

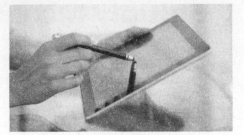

A. Each unit square shown represents a square with a side length of 1 inch. Use this area model to represent the area of Tam's logo.

B. Why does this area model show four unit squares?

_____

_____

C. How did you show the width of $1\frac{1}{3}$ inches?

_____

_____

D. How did you show the length of $1\frac{3}{4}$ inches?

_____

_____

E. How many equal-sized parts represent the area of the logo?

_____

F. What is the area of each equal-sized part? How do you know?

_____

_____

G. What is the area of the logo? Justify your reasoning.

_____

_____

Step It Out

2 Tam makes another logo. The area of the logo is represented by the purple shading.

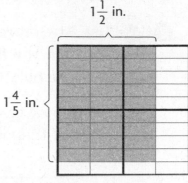

A. How many equal-sized parts represent the area of the logo?

_____

B. Find the area of one equal-sized part.

_____

C. What is the area of the logo? Explain your reasoning. Write an equation to model the problem.

_____

_____

D. Rename $1\frac{1}{2}$ and $1\frac{4}{5}$ as fractions greater than 1.

_____

E. Use your answers from Part D to write an equation to model the area of the logo.

_____

_____

 Turn and Talk How are the equations that model the area of the logo in Parts C and E related? How do they connect to the visual model?

• •

Check Understanding [Math Board]

1 Jonah's new poster has a width of $1\frac{1}{4}$ yards and a length of $1\frac{1}{3}$ yards. Use this area model to represent the area of the poster. What is the area of the poster? Write an equation using fractions greater than 1 to model the problem.

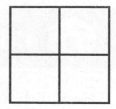

On Your Own

2  **Use Structure** The flagpole at a park is $3\frac{1}{3}$ yards tall. The flagpole at a museum is $1\frac{1}{2}$ times as tall as the height of the flagpole at the park.

- Explain how to write an equation to model the height of the museum's flagpole.

_____

_____

- What is the height of the museum's flagpole?

_____

3 **(MP) Model with Mathematics** Debbie measures the length and the width of a cell phone. The length is $5\frac{3}{5}$ inches, and the width is $2\frac{4}{5}$ inches. What is the area of the front of the cell phone? Write an equation using fractions greater than 1 to model the problem.

_____

Multiply.

4 $2\frac{1}{5} \times 3\frac{1}{2} =$ _____

5 _____ $= 5\frac{1}{2} \times 1\frac{1}{3}$

6 $2\frac{1}{4} \times 1\frac{2}{3} =$ _____

7 **STEM** An early computer connection called USB 1.0 transfers about $1\frac{1}{2}$ megabytes of data each second. A later connection called USB 2.0 transfers data $40\frac{1}{2}$ times as fast as the speed of the USB 1.0. How many megabytes can a USB 2.0 connection transfer

each second? _____

I'm in a Learning Mindset!

How did I use feedback my teacher gave me?

_____

Name _____

Practice Multiplication with Fractions and Mixed Numbers

(I Can) solve a real world problem by writing a multiplication equation to model the problem.

Step It Out

1 ▶ Lara prepares for an upcoming concert. On Saturday, she practiced flute for $2\frac{1}{2}$ hours. On Sunday, she practiced $\frac{1}{2}$ as long as she practiced on Saturday. How long did she practice on Sunday?

A. Write a multiplication equation to model the problem.

_____

B. Without doing any calculations, how do you know whether she practiced more on Saturday or Sunday?

_____

_____

_____

C. Rewrite your equation from Part A so that the mixed number is renamed as a fraction greater than 1. Then solve the equation.

_____

D. How long did Lara practice on Sunday?

_____

 Turn and Talk Lara models the amount of time she practiced on Friday with the equation $\frac{4}{3} \times 2\frac{1}{2} = r$. How does the amount of time she practiced on Friday compare to the amount of time she practiced on Saturday? How do you know?

2 Nick makes a papier mâché black-chinned sparrow for science class. An actual black-chinned sparrow is about $5\frac{3}{4}$ inches long. He makes his sparrow 2 times this size. What is the length of his sparrow?

A. Write a multiplication equation to model the problem.

_____

B. Rewrite your equation from Part A so that the whole number and mixed number are renamed as fractions.

_____

C. Solve your equation from Part B.

_____

D. What is the length of Nick's black-chinned sparrow?

_____

Turn and Talk How can you use the Distributive Property to find the product for your equation from Part A?

• •

Check Understanding `Math Board`

1 The Bucks County Film Festival shows three films. Each film is $1\frac{9}{10}$ hours long. How long are all three films? Write a multiplication equation to model the problem.

_____

Find the product.

2 $5 \times 3\frac{1}{2}$

3 $3\frac{3}{4} \times \frac{1}{3}$

On Your Own

4 (MP) **Model with Mathematics** A fog machine is filled with $1\frac{1}{8}$ quarts of fog liquid at the beginning of a music performance. It needs to be refilled with the same amount after 2 hours. How much fog liquid is put into the fog machine? Write a multiplication equation to model the problem.

_____

Find the product.

5 $5 \times 3\frac{1}{3}$

6 $2\frac{1}{3} \times \frac{1}{4}$

7 $1\frac{3}{4} \times \frac{3}{5}$

_____

8 $4\frac{5}{6} \times 8$

9 $4 \times 4\frac{1}{8}$

10 $2\frac{1}{4} \times 4\frac{3}{4}$

_____

11 (MP) **Model with Mathematics** Mark is $4\frac{1}{3}$ feet tall. His brother Sam is $\frac{3}{4}$ times as tall as he is.

- Write an equation to model Sam's height. Then find

  Sam's height. _____

- Is Sam taller than or shorter than Mark? How do you know?

  _____

  _____

12 (MP) **Attend to Precision** For the next city council election, $1\frac{5}{6}$ times as many candidates are running as had run in the last election. In the last election, 24 candidates ran for the city council. Explain how to use the Distributive Property to find the number of candidates who are running in the next election.

_____

_____

On Your Own

13 A puppy weighs $2\frac{7}{8}$ pounds. Carla feeds the puppy 3 ounces of food for each pound that the puppy weighs. How many ounces of food does Carla feed the puppy? Write a multiplication equation to model the problem.

_____

14 (MP) **Reason** Desiree writes songs for her band. Her first song is $3\frac{1}{2}$ minutes long. Her second song is $1\frac{1}{2}$ times as long as her first song. Her third song is $\frac{2}{3}$ times as long as her second song.

- How many minutes long are the second and third songs?

_____

- What equations did you use to model the length of each song?

_____

_____

15 Brian spends $1\frac{3}{4}$ hours carving the parts for a model airplane. He spends 3 times as long assembling and painting the model. How many hours does Brian spend carving, assembling, and painting the model? Explain how you found your answer.

_____

_____

_____

16 (MP) **Use Repeated Reasoning** To make a batch of lavender paint, three different types of paint are mixed together: $1\frac{1}{2}$ gallons of white, $\frac{1}{2}$ gallon of red, and 2 gallons of blue. Ronald wants to make $2\frac{2}{3}$ batches of lavender paint. How much of each paint color does he need?

_____

Name _____

Apply Fraction Multiplication to Find Area

(I Can) solve multiplication problems with fractions and mixed numbers to find the area of rectangles.

Step It Out

1 ▷ Toni hangs a plaque that is $5\frac{1}{2}$ inches wide and $8\frac{1}{2}$ inches long. How much wall space does the plaque cover?

A. Write an equation to model the problem using fractions greater than 1.

_____

B. Find the product from Part A. What does this product represent?

_____

_____

C. How much wall space does the plaque cover?

_____

D. What units did you use in your answer in Part C? Explain your reasoning.

_____

_____

_____

 Turn and Talk Toni hangs a poster that is $8\frac{1}{2}$ inches wide and 11 inches long. Can the equation $17 \times 11 \div 2 = r$ be used to model the amount of wall space the poster covers? How do you know?

2 ▸ Emma works to clean paintings that have been covered with dust and dirt. She must work very slowly to protect the paint. Last week, she cleaned a painting that has an area of $1\frac{1}{3}$ square yards. This week she cleans a painting that has an area that is $\frac{1}{16}$ the area of the first painting. What is the area of the painting that she cleans this week?

A. Write an equation to model the problem.

_____

B. Solve the equation to find the area of the painting.

_____

C. Is your answer reasonable? How do you know?

_____

_____

_____

Check Understanding [Math Board]

1 Martina builds a pen for rabbits. The pen measures $3\frac{2}{3}$ ft by $4\frac{1}{2}$ ft. What is the area of the pen?

_____

Write an equation to model the area of the rectangle. Find the area.

2

$\frac{1}{2}$ yd

$\frac{3}{8}$ yd

3

$2\frac{1}{5}$ ft

$\frac{3}{4}$ ft

_____   _____

On Your Own

4 The area of a bathroom is 40 square feet. The area of another room is $2\frac{3}{4}$ times as great as the area of the bathroom. What is the area of the other room?

_____

Find the area of the rectangle.

5

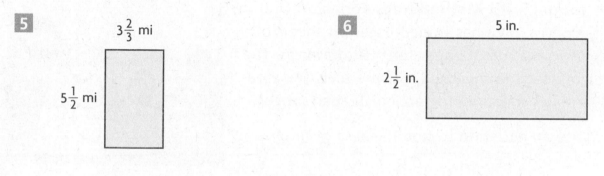

$3\frac{2}{3}$ mi

$5\frac{1}{2}$ mi

6

5 in.

$2\frac{1}{2}$ in.

_____

7 (MP) **Model with Mathematics** Kyra cuts a rectangular piece of wood to make a desktop that is $5\frac{1}{2}$ feet long and $3\frac{1}{8}$ feet wide. What is the area of the desktop? Write an equation to model the area.

_____

8 Ms. Amari compares baking sheets in her restaurant's kitchen. One baking sheet is $2\frac{1}{6}$ feet long and $1\frac{1}{2}$ feet wide. Another baking sheet has the same width, but is $1\frac{1}{12}$ feet long. How much more area does the larger baking sheet have than the smaller baking sheet?

_____

_____

9 A square window has side lengths that are $2\frac{1}{4}$ feet. What is the area of the window?

_____

On Your Own

10 (MP) **Model with Mathematics** Catherine plants flowers in a planter that is $1\frac{3}{8}$ feet wide and $3\frac{1}{2}$ feet long. She plans to cover the entire area with fertilizer. Over how much area will she need to spread the fertilizer? Write an equation to model the area.

_____

11 (MP) **Model with Mathematics** For an art club project, Ms. Davis has students tear off sheets of paper from a roll of paper for their drawings. The area of Teagan's sheet is $3\frac{3}{8}$ square feet. The area of Jerome's sheet is $\frac{1}{2}$ the area of Teagan's sheet.

- Write an equation to find the area of Jerome's sheet of paper.

_____

- What is the area of Jerome's sheet of paper?

_____

12 A flag has a width of $\frac{3}{4}$ yard and a length of $1\frac{1}{4}$ yards. What is its area? Write an equation to model the problem.

_____

13 A rug is $2\frac{3}{5}$ feet wide and 4 feet long. What is its area? Write an equation to model the problem.

_____

14 (MP) **Attend to Precision** A bulletin board is $1\frac{1}{2}$ feet wide and 2 feet long. Gene covers $\frac{3}{8}$ of the bulletin board with blue paper.

- What is the area of the bulletin board? _____

- How many square feet does he cover with blue paper? Write an equation to model the area.

_____

Review

Concepts and Skills

1 What is the area of a rectangular rug with side lengths $2\frac{1}{2}$ feet and $1\frac{1}{2}$ feet? Use the grid to find the area. Let each square represent $\frac{1}{2}$ foot by $\frac{1}{2}$ foot.

_____

2 A closet measures $6\frac{1}{4}$ feet by $3\frac{1}{2}$ feet. How much carpeting is needed to cover the floor of the closet? Use the rectangle to draw an area model to solve.

_____

_____

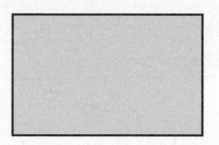

3 **(MP)** **Use Tools** Michael has a piece of wood that is $2\frac{1}{4}$ feet long. He needs a second piece of wood that is $1\frac{1}{2}$ times as long as the first piece. How long is the second piece of wood? Tell what strategy or tool you will use to answer the question, explain your choice, and then find the answer.

(A) $2\frac{1}{8}$ feet   (C) $3\frac{5}{8}$ feet

(B) $3\frac{3}{8}$ feet   (D) $3\frac{3}{4}$ feet

4 Select all the expressions that are equivalent to $4\frac{4}{5}$.

(A) $3 \times 1\frac{3}{5}$

(B) $5 \times 1\frac{2}{5}$

(C) $4 \times 1\frac{1}{5}$

(D) $4 \times 4 \div 5$

(E) $8 \times 3 \div 5$

5 The distance from the campground to the lake is $6\frac{3}{4}$ miles. If Anya has hiked $\frac{2}{3}$ of the way from the campground to the lake, how far is she from the lake?

_____

6 Miguel spends $3\frac{1}{2}$ hours working outside. He spends $\frac{3}{4}$ of the time working in the garden. How much time does he spend working in the garden? Write an equation to model the problem.

_____

7 A closet floor measures $2\frac{1}{2}$ feet by $5\frac{1}{2}$ feet. What is the area of the closet floor?

Ⓐ $10\frac{1}{4}$ square feet

Ⓑ $13\frac{1}{2}$ square feet

Ⓒ $13\frac{3}{4}$ square feet

Ⓓ $27\frac{1}{2}$ square feet

Find the product.

8 $1\frac{1}{3} \times 1\frac{3}{4}$

9 $2\frac{1}{4} \times 3\frac{1}{2}$

_____   _____

10 Select all the equations that can be used to model the area of a piece of rectangular paper that measures $2\frac{1}{3}$ inches by $6\frac{1}{4}$ inches.

Ⓐ $\frac{6}{3} \times \frac{11}{4} = \frac{66}{12}$

Ⓑ $\frac{7}{3} \times \frac{25}{4} = \frac{175}{12}$

Ⓒ $\frac{7}{3} \times 6\frac{1}{4} = 14\frac{7}{12}$

Ⓓ $\frac{5}{3} \times 6\frac{1}{4} = 10\frac{5}{12}$

Ⓔ $2\frac{1}{3} \times \frac{24}{4} = 14$

Ⓕ $2\frac{1}{3} \times 6\frac{1}{4} = 14\frac{7}{12}$

fractions as, 239–242
inverse operation of multiplication, 34–36
partial quotients, 48–50
reasonableness of quotients, 429–432
remainder as fraction, 59–62
with two-digit divisors, 37–42, 43–46, 47–50, 55–58, 59–62, 63–66, 68–70

divisor, 34, 240, 241, 438–441. *See also* division

E

edges, 96

elapsed time, 309–312

equations
addition, 171–174
division, 267–270, 271–274, 275–278, 279–282, 283–286, 287–290
multiplication, 209–212, 225–228, 229–232
subtraction, 172–174

equilateral triangle, 502–504

equivalent fractions, 142–144, 153–156, 161–162, 443–444

estimate
differences, 151–152
products, 17–20, 21–24
quotients, 43–46, 55, 56, 63–66, 429–432, 434–436, 444, 447
sums, 149–152
volume, 103–106

expanded form, 324–325, 389

exponent, 10–12, 371–374, 419, 421–424

exponent form, 10–12

expressions, numerical, 75–78, 79–82, 83–86, 209–212

F

faces, 96

fluid ounce (fl oz), 296, 299, 300

formulas, for volume, 113–116

fractions
addition, 129–132, 133–136, 149–152, 153–156, 167–170

division
by whole numbers, 243–246, 247–252, 279–282, 283–286, 287–290
whole numbers by, 253–256, 257–262, 271–274, 275–278, 287–290
as division, 239–242, 443–444, 446
equivalent, 141–144, 153–156, 161–162, 443–444
multiplication
with area model, 199–204
groups of equal shares, 181–184
by mixed numbers, 225–228, 229–232
products as area representation, 199–204
related equations, 267–270
represent, 191–194, 195–198, 209–212
scaling interpretation of, 205–208,
by whole numbers, 185–190, 209–212
remainders as, 59–62
subtraction, 130–132, 137–140, 151–152, 153–156

G

gallon (gal), 296, 299, 302, 304, 308, 460, 463, 465

geometry
classify figures, 497–500, 501–504, 505–508, 509–512
cubic unit, 95–98, 99–102, 105–106, 107–112
heptagon, 498, 500
hexagon, 497–500
nonagon, 498, 500
parallelogram, 506–508, 509–512
polygon, 497–500, 509–512
quadrilateral, 505–508, 509–512
rectangle, 505–508, 509–511
rhombus, 505–508, 509–512
right rectangular prism, 96, 99–102, 103–106, 107–112, 113–116, 117–122
solid figures, building with unit cubes, 95–98, 99–102
square, 506–508, 509–512
trapezoid, 507–508, 509–512
triangle, 501–504, 509, 511–512
Venn diagram, 497, 509–512
volume, 99–102, 103–106, 107–112, 113–116, 117–122

Index

Mathematical Practices and Processes
1. *make sense of problems and persevere in solving them,* occurs throughout. Some examples are 47, 49, 62, 79, 95, 107, 133, 137, 149, 171, 172, 185, 187, 221, 229, 253, 295, 327, 331, 347, 379, 389, 402, 405, 425, 429, 437, 447, 477, 505
2. *reason abstractly and quantitatively,* in some lessons. Some examples are 12, 20, 24, 28, 78
3. *construct viable arguments and critique the reasoning of others,* in